The safety razor is invented.

The first gasoline-powered farm tractor manufactured.

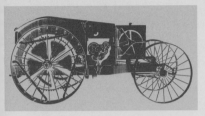

John Schuberg opens Vancouver's Edison Electric Theatre – Canada's first permanent movie-house.

MARVELOUS MOVING PICTURES, clear, sharp and distinct, and just as easy to operate as an ordinary magic lantern. Imagine sitting quietly in your own home and seeing a great railroad train dash by on the screen at a tremendous rate of speed; pulling its long string of swaying Pullmans as it flashes past. You can almost hear the roar of the giant wheels as the train thunders by and vanishes in the distance, leaving a cloud of smoke and dust behind. You can see exciting automobile races, with great crowds of people surging about and pressing back against the lines as the huge cars sweep past like a flash. You can see ocean steamships coming into port, crowds of people moving along the city streets just as natural as life, boys diving from spring boards, and scores of the most amusing comic subjects besides trick films with strange and remarkable effects, all proving a never ending pleasure and amusement to your family and to your friends.

LIFE LIKE PICTURES

SHOW PICTURES ABOUT 4 FEET WIDE

American Federation of Labor becomes dominant force in Canadian labour movement.

1903

Ontario establishes 7 m.p.h. speed limit for motor cars.

Barr Colonists arrive in the District of Saskatchewan.

Boundary arbitration establishes Alaskan border between Canada and the United States.

Roald Amundsen travels the North-West Passage from east to west in the *Gjoa*.

Silver discovered by railway workers near Cobalt, Ont.

Ernest Arthur LeSuer of Sault Ste. Marie patents process for liquification of natural gas.

Henri Bourassa founds *La Ligue Nationaliste Canadienne*.

Turtle Mountain landslide buries Frank, Alta., under 90 million tons of rock; 66 lives lost.

1904

Charles E. Saunders produces disease-resistant, quick-ripening Marquis wheat.

Tommy Ryan of Toronto develops five-pin bowling.

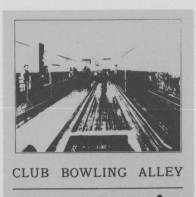

CLUB BOWLING ALLEY

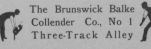

The Brunswick Balke Collender Co., No 1 Three-Track Alley

W. A. INGRAM, Proprietor   Fernie, B. C.

George Lyon of Toronto wins Olympic golf championship.

Earl Grey appointed governor general.

Major section of downtown Toronto destroyed by fire.

Fourteen-year-old violinist Kathleen Parlow of Calgary debuts with the London Symphony.

Operatic soprano Pauline Donalda of Montreal debuts in *Manon* in Nice, France, at age 21.

Into the 20th Century

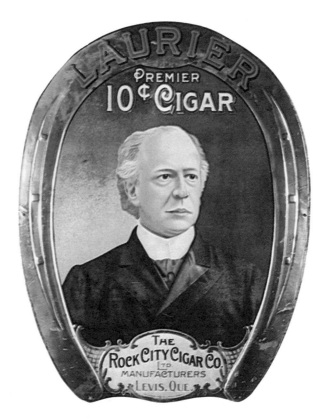

LAURIER

PREMIER
10¢ CIGAR

THE
ROCK CITY CIGAR CO.
LTD
MANUFACTURERS
LEVIS, QUE.

Above: *Prosperity and vitality seem to jump off the* Globe's *colour cover for Christmas, 1901. The world came to Massey-Harris for farm machinery, and Santa still lived.*

Previous page: *This cigar-band shaped trade sign was designed to cash in on the tremendous prestige of the prime minister. He could sell railways to Canada; why not cigars?*

Alan Phillips
Into the 20th Century
1900/1910

Canada's Illustrated Heritage

Canada's Illustrated Heritage

Publisher: Jack McClelland
Editorial Consultant: Pierre Berton
Historical Consultant: Michael Bliss
Editor-in-Chief: Toivo Kiil
Associate Editors: Michael Clugston
     Clare McKeon
     Jean Stinson
Assistant Editors: Julie Dempsey
     Marta Howard
Design: William Hindle
   Lynn Campbell
   Neil Cochrane
Cover Artist: Alan Daniel
Picture Research: Lembi Buchanan
     Michel Doyon
     Judy Forman
     Betty Gibson
     Margot Sainsbury

ISBN: 0-9196-4422-8

N.S.L. Natural Science of Canada Limited
254 Bartley Drive
Toronto, Ontario M4A 1G4

Printed and bound in Canada

This loosely-robed sylph celebrates the man-made dawn of technology.
Electricity was strung into remote corners of the country during the decade,
and changed the style and standards of life of ordinary Canadians.

Contents

Ring in the New Century

Last century made the world a neighbourhood; this century must make it a brotherhood.

J. S. Woodsworth

As evening shadowed London on January 22, 1901, a tired old lady slipped out of the world. Victoria, Queen of England, had ruled one-quarter of the earth, one in every five persons on the planet. One could travel around the globe secure in British law and custom, the nearest thing to a world government that man had ever known. Values were stable, business expansive, and progress was more of the new gospel. Victoria had always tried to keep things as they were, having her husband's hot shaving water brought to his room every morning even though he had died thirty-nine years earlier. But now Victoria was gone, and with her an age.

The new era would be named for her eldest son Bertie, Edward VII. He was self-assured, elegant and buoyant; smug, extravagant and slightly naive. He believed in British imperialism, a unity based on trade (pundits agreed that war was now "economically impossible"); communications (Sir Sandford Fleming, the Canadian surveyor famed for devising standard time, was just completing the trans-Pacific cable); and science (whose latest marvel was the fast "unsinkable" steel steamship). Edward, in faith and temperament, was typical of his time.

It was a time of change - exciting, significant, paradoxical. It was called the age of peace and it nurtured the seeds of the Great War. It was called the age of order and it bred chaos. It was called the Golden Years, the Spirited Years and the Confident Years, yet in its blind optimism were planted the seeds of pessimism.

Change in Canada was guided by Prime Minister Wilfrid Laurier. He headed a dominion of over 5.3 million people, 87 per cent Canadian-born. Most lived on farms or in small communities where they knew almost everyone else, almost everyone went to some church, and the family looked after its own. The major events of the decade were to have a profound effect on these values of community, church and home: events both at home and abroad re-shaped the young dominion.

The optimism that fed imperialism was also nourishing nationalism; the conflicts surrounding nationalism run through the Laurier years. In 1901 the Canadian militia was commanded and armed by Britons. Eight steelclad British cruisers patrolled Canadian fisheries. Canada had no navy; Halifax was a British base. Intelligence reached Laurier through Lord Minto, the governor general, on the rare occasions His Lordship felt it necessary. Canada could not sign treaties; it had no foreign ambassadors.

But by 1910 Laurier had his own chief of staff, the right to sign commercial treaties, and, though

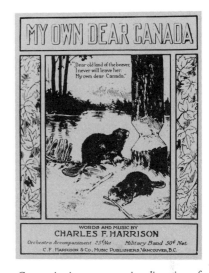

Group singing was a major diversion of the time; the old parlour upright was not there for show. This song mingles beavers with Canadian patriotism.

Opposite page: Two centuries meet in Isaac Erb's photograph of St. John, N.B. An auto and telegraph wires contrast with the arc lamp and horses.

Queen Victoria's death was mourned around the world, and in Belleville, Ont., churches joined in memorial services. While she lived, she seemed remote and half-divine, and she had fostered a cult among British subjects and commanded hysterical loyalty throughout the kingdom. In Quebec, the funeral went unnoticed.

it was only a clearing house for communications from London, an external affairs department. He had a civil service commission, a conservation commission, laboratories for fisheries and mines, an agricultural field service, an Ottawa branch of the Royal Mint, a national observatory. There was also a national archivist although he wasn't given a building till 1912, after irreplaceable documents, including a deed signed by Louis XIV of France, were found scattered in basements and stable lofts, damaged by dampness, heat and mice. The last British warship based at Halifax and Esquimalt had departed with the last British redcoat, leaving Canada protected by a bill to set up a navy. It was enough to make one imperialist. The Honourable George Foster told his fellow Torontonians that Canadians were "getting too bumptious."

The long world-wide depression had ended in 1896. Europe was prospering, it needed bread, and the Canadian northwest was the last undeveloped wheatland in the world. "A new star has risen upon the horizon," Laurier had said. "And it is toward that star that every immigrant . . . now turns his gaze."

the Canadian miracle

They were coming by the tens of thousands, lured by a westerner, Clifford Sifton, who as minister of the interior was staging the biggest, brassiest, most successful immigration pitch in Canadian history. He sent out millions of pamphlets in dozens of languages – none of them mentioning drought, hail, grasshoppers or rust. He strung a net of agents all across northern Europe and hired a shipping line to bring in the catch. Regina grew from two to thirty thousand in the decade, during a boom so wild that in Calgary real estate offices outnumbered grocery stores two to one. In ten years the immigrants quintupled wheat production. It was called "the Canadian miracle," and

so it must have seemed.

Prosperity seemed endless, and the base of that prosperity was the Canadian Pacific Railway, hauling lumber east from British Columbia, cattle and wheat from "the last, best West." No one doubted that more railways meant more prosperity. "The hopper," said CPR chairman William Van Horne, "is too big for the spout."

last great railway era

Wheat was underwriting a last great railway era – last and most profligate. In a moment of frankness in 1899 Sir Edmund Osler, a Toronto financier and CPR director, had called the railways "the main source of corruption in elections . . . It is from such subsidies that the money is supplied to pay the men who have been engaged in the ballot stuffing and the election frauds which we hear so much about."

A man's dream of affluence was a safe stuffed with railway bonds. A boy's dream of greatness was to be a railway president and ride around in a private car like William Mackenzie and Donald Mann, two one-time Ontario farm boys who were lacing a patchwork of shoestring lines into a second transcontinental railway. Some called them the last robber barons, others saw them as public benefactors; in either case their ambitions still affect the Canadian economy.

A hundred-mile rail line north from North Bay uncovered silver at Cobalt; the money coined from silver financed the continent's richest gold camp and gave Toronto the world's biggest mining market.

It was a dynamic period; a cigar-box maker from Baden, Ontario, made good his promise to supply cheap electrical power across the province. Adam Beck fought the powerful private power firms, eventually buying them out, and ensured the early success of Ontario Hydro. In the heyday of private enterprise he championed public ownership of the utility, making powerful enemies in the business community.

Education was not yet a major force for change. University was for the rich and many opposed public education. Higher education was impractical; this was as widely accepted as the uselessness of art. Only a few saw education as the corrective for social injustice, and fewer still were working toward those ends, but those who were, such as J. S. Woodsworth and Henry Marshall Tory, had an impact far beyond their time.

The optimism of the era did not extend to aviation, although these were aviation's critical years, when a group of young men in Cape Breton, financed by Mabel Bell, led the continent in promoting flight, at the time flight needed it most. And not even Bell had an inkling that his hilltop home at Baddeck would be the chrysalis of Canada's aircraft industry.

It was the spring of Canadian capitalism. In the two years following 1909, 41 corporations would swallow up 196 small separate companies.

In 1910 five companies were merged in the Steel Company of Canada, and Cyrus Birge, its vice president, declared "We not only manufacture steel, we manufacture nationalism." In 1900 society had been unified by belief: in the righteousness of work, in the sanctity of marriage, and in man as the chosen instrument of God's will. By 1910 it was moving toward a new unity.

reshaping their world

These were the main currents of the decade: variations on the theme of change, though the heroes of most of these stories were working less for change than for growth. To them, as to Queen Victoria, growth meant more and more of the same. Few realized that the events they were shaping would remake the world as they knew it, from its foundation of faith to its life styles.

Railways and mines made Sandon, B.C., a minor boom town at the turn of the century. As if their long shifts weren't tough enough, on a 1904 holiday these miners held – what else – a drilling contest.

CHAPTER ONE

Hometown, Canada

The woman who exclaims, "The Dickens," or "Mercy," or "Goodness" when she is annoyed or astonished, is vulgar in spirit.

Our Deportment, John H. Young

Canada was still a nation in which the frontier was never far from the city and the regions were as insular as the semi-colonial psyche. Maritime farmers hauled wood with oxen and their wives carded wool for yarn, while Sydney was an industrial centre thriving on coal and steel. Montreal was a great world port with raucous taverns and Louis Quinze churches where some forty millionaires lived on Sherbrooke Street in one "Golden Mile." But areas of rural Quebec had slumbered on for a century without changing. Wooden mansions were rising in Winnipeg, but westward in "the territories" immigrants lived in huts of sod, weaving cloth from fibres of flax, decorating it with embroidery and colouring it with homemade yellow and red dyes. British Columbia was a land apart, a region of isolated ranches, logging camps, mining camps, cannery towns and fruit farms. Vancouver was American, Victoria more English than England, and the rivalry even more acute than that between Calgary and Edmonton.

More than half the people lived on farms and another quarter in small towns but they had little in common with each other. The farmer rose at dawn and finished his chores by lamplight. He butchered his own meat, churned his own butter, grew his own fruit and vegetables. If he prospered he painted his barn, then he added a porch to his house, then he bought his wife a piano and then he sent one son to college.

On Saturday he hitched up the team and drove his family to town in the "democrat." He bought sacks of flour and oatmeal, molasses, beans and dried fruit, maybe a bolt of cloth for the wife and some jawbreakers for the kids. He mingled with townsfolk at band concerts, the fall fair, seed fair, or cattle show, the travelling medicine show or the one-ring circus, and now and then in the town hall at a euchre night or a square dance. But he was always a man apart, a hayseed in store clothes.

But already the farmer's work horse was being replaced by the small gas tractor, enlarging the acreage that he could work, while easing his job. As Doc Kelley of Uxbridge, Ontario, "King of the Medicine Men," said later, bemoaning the passing of his trade, "There's just no such thing as a si-mon-pure, dyed-in-the-wool rube any more."

People were divided, not only by region and work, but by class. One dressed according to one's station. Most townsmen, at least on Sunday, wore high starched collars, detachable shirt cuffs, a derby hat called a "bowler," or a summer straw called a "boater." Men of affairs wore high silk hats called "toppers," fur-collared overcoats, swallow-tailed frock coats, waistcoats draped with gold

Romance and maple leaves pulled at Canadian heart-strings as early as 1901, when this song was written.

Opposite page:The LaPrell home was thought the finest in 1902 Edmonton. Its parlour fittings were hallmarks of the period: piano, wicker chairs, tasseled portière and yards of drapery.

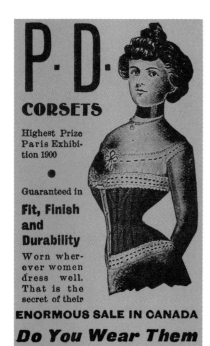
"Wasp waist" corsets tested the constitutions of stout women. Ladies could pinch their mid-sections with the dip hip, gored hip or fan front styles; stouter forms called for steel or bone reinforcing.

The shoes and boots – high or low, buttoned or laced – and the spotless salesmen in their stiff linen collars seem equally on display in this St. John, N.B., shoe store. Potted palms were everywhere in the 1900s. Clearly an up-to-date management.

chains and striped trousers that "broke" on the instep of their high boots. Others wore sack suits of grades that gave a man's standing at a glance.

Women were swathed in layer on layer of cloth – drawers, corset, corset cover, petticoat, chemise – and sheathed in a dress that almost brushed the cobblestones, though by the decade's end it had risen to the ankle. Getting in and out of cars made women impatient with hampering clothes; they were talking of freedom in dress, though in 1910 a bloomer display in a Regina department store nearly caused a riot. In 1905 the "wasp waist" was "in." Poorer women wore it in cotton; "ladies" displayed it in lace, silk, velvet and satin, and embellished it with huge hats of ostrich plumes, feathered boas, furs and parasols – the impractical dress of those with nothing to do but ring for a servant.

Some of the rich aspired to be aristocrats. They were conspicuous consumers. They drove to work in lacquered coaches with footmen. They built homes that resembled chateaux, capped with cupolas, towers and turrets, adorned with balconies, dormers, spindles, scrollwork and stained glass. Some had ballrooms, built-in organs, elevators, fountains, conservatories. They competed in their social life as in business. Montreal financier James Ross staffed his mansion with fifty servants. Toronto merchant John Eaton, a yachtsman, maintained a private wireless station. CPR chairman William Van Horne displayed paintings worth $3 million.

If the rich were princes, the well-to-do were squires. An upper-middle-class lady had electric light in her house, running water, a water closet, a cast iron bathtub with claw feet, a telephone, central hot-water heating, an icebox, a carpet sweeper, a gas range with a head-high warming oven, a washing machine that was cranked by hand and a

The Van Wart Brothers tended to the gastronomic needs of St. John, N.B., from their corner grocery store. Bacon sold for 27¢ a pound, and $6 bought 100 pounds of sugar. The sauerkraut barrel foretold the weather – stormy if the cabbage rose in the brine.

"Good morning, nurse."
"Good Morning, Doctor."
"What news this morning?"
"Six died during the night."
"How is that? I though I prescribed 'Vin tonique' for seven."
"Yes, but that fellow in the corner refused to take it — he is drinking

WILSON'S INVALIDS' PORT."

Alcohol was still the main cure-all for any ailment. This heavy-handed sales pitch promises extended, if tipsy, life.

sewing machine pumped by foot. She managed a house with a drawing room, sitting room, sun room, sewing room, guest room and a hired girl who "lived in" for $12 a month.

The average housewife lit the kerosene lamp and the woodstove in the morning. She melted snow for water or primed the backyard pump. She washed with a pitcher and basin and emptied the water into a slop pail. She browned her toast with a fork over the fire. She shopped every day, scrubbed clothes on a washboard, wrung them and hung them outside, beat the carpets with a wire whip, baked bread, put up preserves and bathed weekly after the children in a tin tub in the kitchen.

Many people were still afraid of being poisoned by canned food. But diseases of stress and tension – heart disease and psychoneurosis, uncommon the previous century – were replacing typhoid (which in 1905 had killed 1,906 people in Winnipeg). Montreal led the battle against typhoid with a sewage plant in 1909. X-rays were revolutionizing surgery, and they also showed that the skull of Jack Johnson, who had beaten Canada's Tommy Burns for the heavyweight championship of the world in 1908, was thicker than the skull of a Texas steer. Psychologists were exploring the mind, biologists the glands, and Arthur Keith, a Canadian professor, predicted that plain people would be made beautiful by treatment of the pituitary gland.

In the cities immigrants lived in slums, worked in basement and attic factories. Sanitation was poor, ventilation worse. Women sewed in perpetual twilight. Some nine-year-olds worked ten hours a day, six days a week, without vacation. The average wage in industry was $400 a year.

The sexes were as segregated as the classes. For a lady to enter a bowling alley or public house was

Woman's Work

Work for domestics in private homes was pure drudgery: long hours, lack of social freedom and privacy, and negligible pay. So when factories and offices began to spring up, many women left their maid's aprons for a steady wage and some freedom. But their rise in fortunes was limited: their jobs were classified "women's work", a slot which always justified low pay. Even the upper-class women's jobs, teaching and nursing, paid poorly.

Afternoon tea was a ritual enjoyed only by the affluent. These Victoria "ladies" sport embroidered waists and their gents puff stogies at a genteel distance.

Not only were their working conditions grim, but these scullery maids in Victoria, B.C., had to live with the low social standing of their job.

Party lines were the rule in the early days of the telephone. These Bell Telephone operators did all the "dialing" for callers, under the supervisor's watchful eye.

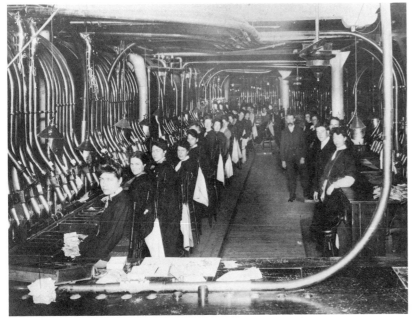

Before cash registers were used at Eaton's, a customer's bill and money were shot down pneumatic tubes to this cash office, where women sent the change back up.

Menial jobs like seamstress would keep bread on the table, but they held little security for old age. That could only come with a "good" marriage.

15

The navy schottische? The ripple? Maybe the bronco? Certainly not the maypole dance. No, it looks as if the pianist on the balcony has these Vancouver dancers doing the Gaby glide.

unthinkable. "She will not go alone to the concert hall or the theatre," noted a visiting British journalist, "even with the man to whom she is engaged, nor will she receive gentlemen alone in her drawing room."

Professional status for women was uncommon. Doctors like Margaret Gordon and Augusta Stowe-Gullen were curiosities; men were still quoting Samuel Johnson, who had likened an educated woman to a dog walking on its hind legs. Women could work in stores and factories; country girls became city servants; but "nice" girls had to choose between nursing and teaching – music, school or elocution. Toronto's two big "Schools of Expression" charged fees as high as university for four years of training in impassioned reading and pantomime. But graduates could charge $6 a lesson, equivalent to a week's pay for a bank clerk, and pros like Pauline Johnson played "opera houses" from coast to coast.

actresses were "fast"

The stage was open to women, and more people saw live theatre than would ever see it again. Three hundred stock companies were on tour across North America with stars like Marie Dressler of Cobourg and little Gladys Smith of Toronto, whose name had not yet been changed to Mary Pickford. But the stage was "immoral" and actresses were "fast," unless, of course, they made $3,150 a week like Lillian Russell.

Only seventy-two women worked for Laurier's government in 1901 and they were shut up in private rooms for fear that the men would corrupt them. Most girls stayed at home and helped mother until the right man came along.

The new syndicated comic strips – Mutt and Jeff, Bringing Up Father – portrayed a world in which men and women still lived apart, mentally and morally. The Dominion Election Act decreed that "No woman, idiot, lunatic or criminal shall vote." A votes-for-women bill was drafted in Ontario in 1910, only to be withdrawn the following year. Premier James Whitney explained "The country is not yet ready for social revolution." A Nova Scotia farmer's wife summed up the general female attitude: "If there's one thing John can do alone, for goodness' sake let him do it!"

But the base for feminism was being laid. Doctors Stowe-Gullen and Gordon, along with Mrs. Flora Denison, had launched the Canadian Women's Suffrage Association. In 1900 Mrs. Margaret Murray had founded the Imperial Order of the Daughters of the Empire, giving women another potent political voice. Emily Murphy, writing under the pseudonym of Janey Canuck, was campaigning for women's rights in Edmonton. And the Winnipeg Women's Press Club, led by Nellie McClung, author of the 1908 bestseller *Sowing Seeds In Danny*, was battling for women's rights in Manitoba.

romance on a bicycle

Segregation extended into sport. An aura of fashion surrounded golf, croquet and tennis. Skiing was expensive, a European novelty. Basketball, invented only nine years before by James Naismith, an expatriate Canadian, was known only to university students. Tobogganing called for a club membership and most of the clubs had a waiting list. Montreal's Park Slide, where six chutes dropped you a half-mile in forty-five seconds, was usually thronged. Mark Twain, aging but active, went down once and said afterward that he wouldn't have missed it for $100 and wouldn't repeat it for $1,000.

On summer Sundays the roads were dusty with thousands of cyclists, and thousands more wheeled up and down on the paved streets of towns and cities. One in every twelve persons had a "wheel." Some eighty-five cycling magazines were on sale in Canada. Cycles were more than transportation, they were romance. Couples honeymooned on them. Bike races made front-page news. Bicycles lured so many from church that ministers were alarmed: "You cannot serve God and skylark on a bicycle."

the church stood guard

Four churches – Catholic, Methodist, Presbyterian and Anglican – claimed 85 per cent of the population, and all but one-tenth of one per cent of the rest belonged to some sect. The church stood guard over art, education and morals. Silence surrounded all sexual matters. From Confederation till 1901, only fifty-three couples had suffered the shame of divorce. Many teachers were clergymen. The bestselling novel of 1901 – 10,000 copies, heralding "a new era in publishing" – was *The Man from Glengarry* by Ralph Connor, pseudonym of the Reverend Charles Gordon.

Culture was still derivative but "the new voice in Canadian letters," proclaimed Professor Pelham Edgar, would be "a world voice." And indeed the realistic animal stories of Ernest Thompson Seton were an original Canadian *genre,* copied by Kipling. Ralph Connor, "the sky pilot," became so popular in the United States that police were called out to control crowds at his lectures. And in 1910 Stephen Leacock became "the Mark Twain of the British Empire" with *Literary Lapses,* published at his own risk, and against the advice of his journalist friend B. K. Sandwell who thought it would ruin Leacock's reputation as an economist.

Canadians were conservative; tradition was strong. But the channels for new ideas were being formed. In 1901 an organization called the Reading Camp Association, later to be known as Frontier College, was born of an idea that teachers should go to students who cannot come to them. The Association carried free education to the rail-

**Eva Tanguay
The "I Don't Care" Girl**

She was the naughty sensation of the vaudeville stage, the highest-paid actress in America by 1912. Eva Tanguay was born in 1878 in Marbleton, Que., the daughter of a doctor. She made her debut at age eight in "Little Lord Fauntleroy," and toured five years with a stage company. She was a striking woman – risqué, outspoken and outrageous. A show called *The Chaperones* made her a star in 1904; hit songs like "I Don't Care," and "Go as Far as You Like," delivered with slinky movements and suggestive dances, made her the sex goddess of the era. She introduced a new style of dancing and singing which outraged most censors and parents in the 1920s. John Ford was one of her three husbands. In the '29 crash her $2 million fortune went down the drain and her health soon followed. She died, all but forgotten, in 1947.

Champions

Tom Longboat's career as a long-distance runner lasted only six years, but in his prime he was the best in the world. He was raised on Ontario's Six Nations Reserve and emerged as a top runner in 1906. Despite his taste for whiskey and distaste for training he won the Boston Marathon in 1907, then dominated the professional circuit until 1912. He died, forgotten, in 1949.

Tommy Burns was the only Canadian to win the world heavyweight boxing crown, and the first champion to cross the colour line, losing his title to the black American Jack Johnson in 1908. He was born Noah Brusso, and raised near Hanover, Ont. He taunted opponents with distracting insults, then knocked them senseless. The title-holder at 25, he retired with only four losses in 52 fights.

Canadian Bill Sherring's marathon win at the 1906 Olympics created an immense, if short-lived, enthusiasm for long-distance racing. This race is in Cape Breton, N.S.

A shady looking crowd watches while two boxers warm up. When these Victoria, B.C., fighters stepped into the ring for the real thing they wore gloves.

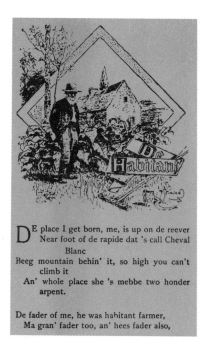

D^E place I get born, me, is up on de reever
　　Near foot of de rapide dat 's call Cheval
　　　Blanc
Beeg mountain behin' it, so high you can't
　　climb it
An' whole place she 's mebbe two honder
　　arpent.

De fader of me, he was habitant farmer,
　　Ma gran' fader too, an' hees fader also,

William Henry Drummond tried to catch the accent of French-Canadian backwoodsmen in his poems. Many Quebecois objected to the idiom, but Louis Frechette, the poet laureat, liked it.

Ernest Thompson Seton's animal stories combine the knowledge of a woodsman and naturalist with an artist's eye. He drew many illustrations for his own books.

way, mining and lumber camps. Around the same time Andrew Carnegie, the enormously wealthy American steel man who had just created the idea of the charitable foundation, donated $425,915 to build libraries in seven Canadian cities. The "free libraries" boosted interest in literature and school among some Canadians; the richer, better-educated gained the most from this "charity".

Then in 1902 Johnny Nash (christened John Schuberg) opened the Edison Electric Theatre on Cordova Street in Vancouver, Canada's first permanent movie house. Five years later, Ernest Ouimet opened the world's first deluxe cinema, a thousand-seat Montreal house that challenged the stage with such innovations as advance sales, reserved seats, a checkroom, intermission and a six-piece orchestra with singers. That same year Julie Allen and his family came to Brantford, Ontario, opened a theatre in a store with 150 kitchen chairs, and within a few years had 50 movie theatres, some deluxe, the first real national chain in North America. In Boston, Louis Mayer, late of Saint John, New Brunswick, was running a little theatre that in eight years he would parlay into the world's biggest factory for the mass-production of values, Metro-Goldwyn-Mayer.

People still gathered around the piano but the world was reaching into the home with the flat black discs of the Victor Talking Machine Company and the coloured slides of the gas-powered magic lantern. And, in 1901, at what would be known as Signal Hill in St. John's, Newfoundland, a young Irish-Italian from England, Guglielmo Marconi, had picked from the air the letter "S" (". . ."), sent from a wireless station in Cornwall, England, thus proving that radio waves followed the curvature of the earth.

In Cape Breton, Marconi was met by Alex Johnston, editor of the Sydney *Daily Record*. Johnston found Marconi disheartened. His experiment was a success but development was blocked by the Anglo-American Cable Company, holder of a trans-Atlantic monopoly. Johnston set up a cabinet interview and Marconi came back from Ottawa with a government grant of $80,000. He built a wireless station at Glace Bay, Nova Scotia. From here, in 1902, Marconi established official trans-Atlantic wireless communication. With further advances in radio technology, mass entertainment for the home was just around the corner.

People in 1910 lived much as they had in 1900. They were still divided by region, church and class, still segregated by sex and education. But developments were underway that in time would dissolve most physical differences and create new life-styles organized around differences in thought.

THE BIOGRAPHY OF A GRIZZLY
by
ERNEST THOMPSON SETON

Bestsellers of the 20th Century

Robert Service
The Backroom Balladeer

Robert Service breathed life into "Dangerous Dan McGrew," cloaked him with a sinister reputation, then had him "pumped full of lead," creating probably the best-known villain in Canadian literature. He emigrated from Scotland to America as a young man, and in 1904 followed the gold dust trail to the Yukon, where he took on a job as Bank of Commerce clerk in Dawson. The gold rush was over but Service mined the stories and legends of the frontier, turning them into volume after volume of verse. His first two books, *Songs of a Sourdough* and *The Spell of the Yukon* (1907), rocketed him to world-wide fame and fortune, and it is said that no writer of the time sold as many books in his lifetime. Before he died in 1958, he wrote over 20 books.

L.M. Montgomery
Lucy of Green Gables

Mark Twain described her classic *Anne of Green Gables* as "the dearest, and most lovable child in fiction since the immortal Alice," and millions of readers all around the world have agreed. Lucy Maud Montgomery was born in Clifton, P.E.I., in 1874. Her mother died when she was a child and her father went west, leaving her with her grandparents. Before her success as a novelist she taught school, wrote colums for the *Halifax Chronicle*, and paid the rent by writing stories for Canadian and American magazines. *Anne* was published in 1908, and for the next 30 years Lucy Maud continued to turn fictionalized reminiscences of her childhood into bestsellers. She wrote 23 books, some of which have been made into films and musicals.

Gilbert Parker
The Master of Romance

He never visited the Northwest, had little understanding of the life of French Canadians, and left Canada for good in 1885, but Horatio Gilbert Parker was the most prolific and popular novelist writing about Canada in the era. Born near Kingston, U.C. (Ont.), in 1862, he studied at the U of T and was ordained in the Anglican Church before going to Australia and finally settling in England. The first of his 40 books, *Pierre and His People: Tales of the Far North* (1892), went through 27 editions in 20 years and set the style for his quaint and sentimental historical romances about Quebec and the wild west. He served as MP in Parliament for 20 years while basking in literary glory, but today only one of his books is in print.

Ralph Connor
The Man From Glengarry

In 1896, Rev. Charles Gordon, the pastor in a run-down church near Winnipeg, wrote a simple story about life in a B.C. lumber camp. He sent the story to the Presbyterian church paper under a pseudonym. Four years later "Ralph Connor" was one of the bestselling authors in the world. He was born in Glengarry, C.W. (Ont.), in 1869, entered the ministry at 30, and served in church missions in the West. A stirring preacher, he wore his kilt in the pulpit, and roused the navvies, cowboys and miners in his congregations with his guitar playing and singing. But he is best known for his novels *The Sky Pilot* and *The Man From Glengarry*. Sales of his 29 books exceed 5 million. During WW I he served as chaplain, and in the 1920s moderated the controversial union of the Protestant churches into the United Church.

This stylish turn-of-the-century couple kept their suede and patent footwear dry with Daisy Rubbers from the Berlin (Ontario) Rubber Manufacturing Company. Both men and women in the decade wore high-buttoned or -laced shoes in the fall and winter, and low pumps in the spring and summer.

Tea was more than a beverage, according to the cat family's testimonial for W.L. Temple of Halifax.

Colourful Come-Ons

Although the new century heralded the dawn of modern technology, advertising by trade card remained the merchant's best promotion.

Today, Avery Buckley's advertising would be in poor taste.

This Halifax haberdasher's trade card was typical in making blacks the butt of humour.

Flies a problem? Wilson's Fly Pads "knock 'em dead" by the bushel.

In 1901, when Dutch settlers were fighting British troops thousands of miles from Canada in the Boer War, Canadians were singing "For home and country let us arm and boldly face the blast" in this patriotic song. Apparently W.N. Harris, "Toronto's favourite baritone," made it a hit.

CHAPTER TWO

A Day in the Life of Laurier

We should have the right to say to Great Britain: if you want us to help you, call us to your councils . . . .

Prime Minister Laurier

On October 12, 1899, Wilfrid Laurier rose as usual at eight o'clock. He shaved and brushed his hair, now at fifty-seven a silvery halo; selected a white-edged waistcoat and knotted his ascot with the care that made him the best-dressed man in the Commons. In the sunny kitchen of the big house that his wealthy backers had bought him, the maid served him tea, one poached egg, one slice of bread without butter.

At nine o'clock his secretary arrived and he read the letters, methodically piling them, turning the pile, dictating his answers. At ten-thirty he caught a carriage to Parliament Hill, conscious that people turned on the street to stare. He was always on stage, aware of his role: in Quebec the hero; in Ontario the phenomenon, the Catholic who had fought his church and changed the course of politics, remodelling Tory Quebec as a Liberal stronghold, the man who came out of a static, seventeenth-century Quebec tradition to lead Canadians into a century of change.

The people crowding his ante-room rose as he came in – tall, graceful, courteous and smiling, always smiling no matter what his thoughts. They filed into his office: politicians seeking jobs for supporters, businessmen soliciting government contracts, unionists asking for a "fair wage law" and a forty-eight-hour week. Some days there were as many as a hundred. He talked to them from a chair that lowered his height to that of his visitors.

His secretary interrupted: a message from the governor general. Laurier opened it with foreboding. Shots exchanged in South Africa. So it *was* war.

Laurier called the cabinet meeting, dreading the conflict he would face. For the first time he regretted the strength of his "ministry of all talents" – Clifford Sifton, who held the west, and the two former provincial premiers, William Fielding of Nova Scotia and Andrew Blair of New Brunswick. In their strength they were independent, and Anglo-Saxons all, brought up like their voters on English history and literature. They believed in the white man's burden and Rule Britannia! Britain's war with the Boers would be their war.

Tension rose in the meeting as Israel Tarte took his seat. It was Tarte who three years before had masterminded the Liberal comeback after eighteen years out of power. In that campaign the French Canadian leaders had had to walk a tightrope between French and English on the Manitoba School question. Now the rope would be drawn even tighter, for Tarte and most Quebeckers were solidly opposed to the idea of a war to help extend Britannia's rule.

Cartoonist Spy of Britain's Vanity Fair *caught a dapper PM Laurier at the 1902 London Colonial Conference.*

Prime Minister Laurier campaigns in the 1908 election. The Liberal slogan was simply "Let Laurier continue his work," and the 67-year-old PM won for the last time in his career.

Now, Laurier again found himself fighting those who wanted no part of the war and those who wanted an all-out effort. He was in the middle, fighting even his own feelings. He, too, sympathized with the Boers, a minority in South Africa, like the French in Canada. He, too, resented the power of Lord Minto, the governor general, and the person of Colonel Edward Hutton, British commander of Canada's militia. Hutton had had an article planted in the *Canadian Military Gazette* stating that, if war began, Canada would send troops. Laurier had cried "pure invention" and straddled the fence with a statement – breaking his custom of no newspaper interviews – that "though we may be willing to contribute troops," it was up to Parliament to decide. The British colonial secretary, Joseph Chamberlain, professed not to hear and accepted an offer that had not been made. It complicated the problem now as Laurier entreated his ministers not to tear apart the party and the nation.

Quebec Liberals on edge

Slowly, sullenly, they compromised. But the next evening, in a last angry protest, a group of Quebec Liberals called at Laurier's office. He presented an Order-in-Council embodying the compromise: one thousand "volunteers," no official contingent. They passed it around with shrugs and weak jokes to Henri Bourassa, the slight, handsome grandson of Louis Joseph Papineau, rebel leader of 1837.

Bourassa stiffened. "Mr. Laurier, do you take account of opinion in Quebec?" Bourassa was a back-bencher, brilliant but young, only thirty-one, a Laurier protégé.

Laurier smiled. "My dear Henri, Quebec doesn't have opinions, only sentiments."

Bourassa probed, an inquisitor, self-righteous, irritating.

Laurier's lips thinned. "The circumstances are difficult."

"To govern is to have courage . . . to risk power to save a principle," Bourassa replied.

The sudden silence was tense. No one had proved his courage more often than Laurier, son of a habitant surveyor. He rose to his feet, his eyes angry. With an effort he regained control. He smiled, walked around his desk and put his hand on Bourassa's shoulder. "Ah, my dear young friend, you have not a practical mind."

Bourassa condemns Laurier

Bourassa edged away; five days later he resigned his seat. When he ran again as an Independent, Laurier did not oppose him – he warned only of a cleavage of the races. But the voice of Bourassa, passionate and shrill, condemning his prime minister for aiding a war of conquest, personified an insular Quebec.

The war, condemned in Europe, was followed with pride in English Canada, which pressured Laurier to send more troops, seven thousand in all. "We claim the rights of British subjects," Laurier explained his acquiescence. "We assume all the responsibilities this entails." But the troops would serve as a Canadian unit, he insisted, rather than enlist in Britain's army. And he forced a reluctant Lord Minto to send home the over-zealous Hutton, another milestone in his slowly-shaping policy of independence.

War was again the issue in the election of 1900, an election fought in the open space outside the Quebec village churches and in public debate at monster rallies in the cities. In Quebec the Tory chief, Sir Charles Tupper, declared that "Sir Wilfrid Laurier is too English for me," that Laurier's "imperialist" speeches at the last Colonial conference had involved Canadians in this imperial war. And in Ontario, Tupper declared that Laurier was "not half British enough," that he had sent too few men to the Boer war too late.

Laurier toured Ontario in his private railway car with its velvet draperies, ornate scrollwork and crystal chandeliers, and spoke on crowded Grand Trunk platforms in the high mellifluous voice that could make talk of tariffs sound like poetry. In Galt he was introduced for the first time to fifteen supporters and as his train was leaving in a cloud of flying cinders he called good-bye to each of them by name.

But his virtuoso performance was in vain. The voting ended with an almost solidly Tory Ontario confronting an almost solidly Liberal Quebec. The West and the Maritimes kept Laurier in power. Reporting to London on Laurier's victory, Lord Minto wrote: "The writing of the leading Opposition papers in Ontario has been positively wicked, simply aiming at stirring up hatred of French Canada."

Minto was a soldier. But he sympathized with Laurier while suspecting, and warning Joseph Chamberlain in London, that "he dreams of Canadian independence in some future age." The colonial secretary disbelieved it, or ignored it. Chamberlain was the hub of a well-financed and influential movement to reshape the empire as a single globe-girdling state, one-fifth of the world linked by blood, language and law. Canada was the cornerstone of the overseas empire and Laurier, the most famous colonial statesman, was the pivot.

"Safety lies in freedom"

Laurier arrived at London's Cecil Hotel for the 1902 Colonial conference feeling ill, weary and uneasy. At the previous conference five years before he had been wined and dined by the aristocracy, given an unwanted knighthood and subjected to, he said, "an incessant and unrelenting imperialist campaign." His disquiet now deepened as he lis-

Armand Lavergne
Laurier's Radical Disciple

Young Armand Lavergne's solution to old problems at the beginning of the century was "throw the English into the St. Lawrence." He entered politics as a 24-year-old MP from Montmagny in 1904 and allied himself with Henri Bourassa in the cause of Quebec *nationalisme*. When and wherever he saw a threat to French culture and language rights, he let go a blast of hyperbole and passion.When Ontario's French schools were closed in 1916, he recommended taking arms against the "Boche" in Ontario before fighting the Germans in Europe. He was a lifelong friend of PM Laurier, but politically the two were poles apart. He served in politics, on and off, until his death in 1935. In Quebec Lavergne is seen as one of the century's first advocates of separatism.

Torontonians jam the streets on June 5, 1901 – Pretoria Day – to celebrate the end of the Boer War. Men under boaters, derbys, fedoras and caps, and women in white shirtwaists push the latest in bicycles complete with coaster brakes and balloon tires. Overhead signs advertise corsets and help for "complexions." Flags wave everywhere.

tened to Chamberlain's opening speech: "Bloodshed has cemented the British Empire.... I cannot conceal . . . very great anticipations" of forming "a new government with large powers of taxation and legislation over countries separated by thousands of miles. . . . Safety lies in unity."

Safety, Laurier answered, lies in freedom. He said no to support for the British navy; Canada would prefer her own navy. No, also, to a permanent imperial secretariat; it would encroach on the "self-governing powers." Laurier spoke for all the colonies; the war that had swelled imperial sentiment had also quickened nationalism.

Chamberlain did not understand; he saw only a stubborn foreigner. At a dinner where Lady Minto called Laurier "a very great gentleman," Chamberlain sniffed: "I would sooner do business with a cad who knows his own mind." He threatened to cancel the fast steamer service planned for Canada. With chill hauteur he told Laurier that he was "a very imperfectly assimilated Englishman." Laurier suggested Chamberlain dine with his English Canadian ministers, and Chamberlain was dismayed to find them Canadians first, imperialists second.

"British to the core"

Over and over Laurier spoke of union for peace, union in freedom, drawing ever closer to the concept of a commonwealth. Visiting France, England's old adversary, he was faced with his statement that he was "British to the core." In his answer he articulated his creed: "We are faithful to the great nation which gave us life [France]. We are faithful to the great nation which gave us liberty [England] . . ."

He came back to Canada so ravaged by asthma that Robert Borden, now opposition leader, averted his gaze. In Laurier's absence, Israel Tarte had been angling for his job, trying to make private deals with the railways, enraging the cabinet by promising manufacturers higher tariffs. Tarte thought he held Quebec; he was campaigning for Ontario. "Laurier," he was reported to have said, "is better loved, but I have the great interests behind me."

Laurier summoned Tarte on the day after his return. No explanations, no apologies, Tarte was out. "I shall be master of Canada," Laurier had once said, "as long as I have Tarte and Sifton with me." Now he had Sifton.

two provinces born

By 1905 the explosive growth on the plains, where the North-West Mounted Police, still in pith helmets, were patrolling boom towns and wheat stubble, forced Laurier to bring in bills creating the provinces of Alberta and Saskatchewan. The bills were highly controversial, especially an education clause that restored the system of separate schools for Protestants and Catholics. Sifton was opposed to separate schools. He had been on vacation in Florida when Laurier introduced the bills, and when he returned he resigned. Laurier could neither dissuade him nor bluff him by threatening to retire. It was Laurier who had to yield, to revise the act, to placate Quebec, to withstand the ire of Henri Bourassa and his new *Ligue Nationaliste.*

Laurier now held his party together by personal prestige. When he spoke the House benches were packed, every page stood at attention and the ticking of the clock could be heard in the chamber. None of the 1908 election scandals or gifts to MPs and ministers in return for timber and land rights outweighed Laurier's reputation. He had created a personality cult the equal of Sir John A. Macdonald's in a nation now twice as big and far more complex.

He was still fighting imperialism. In London in 1907 he had parried demands by a new empire

Among the heroes of the Boer War was Lord Baden-Powell, a British officer who founded the boy scouts movement in 1908. This was the first war in which Canadian troops went overseas. The cost was 224 Canadians dead, 252 wounded.

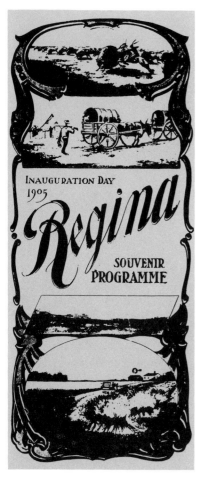

This cover decorated a program for the Sept. 4, 1905, inauguration ceremonies, when Saskatchewan became a province. Three days earlier, to the cannonade of a four-gun battery, Alberta had entered Confederation as a province

advocate, a brash young under-secretary named Winston Churchill. Imperialism flared again in 1909 with the admiralty's warning that within three years Germany's navy would equal Britain's. Laurier now proposed the Canadian navy he had suggested in London in 1902. He preferred it, he said, to paying upkeep for Britain's navy – "colonial tribute." He was supported by the Conservatives, by all the House but Bourassa. The admiralty was shocked, Canadian imperialists called it treason, and Tory leader Robert Borden soon reversed himself.

In Quebec a group of young intellectuals and clerics led by Bourassa teamed up with the Tories in a 1910 by-election to defeat Laurier's candidate, picturing Laurier as the tool of British press-gangs. Outside the office of *Le Devoir* – of which Bourassa was founder and editor – a great crowd gathered to hear the isolationist leader: "I say to you French Canadians that we have today done a great work. We have taught Sir Wilfrid Laurier that he is not omnipotent..." Bourassa resented Laurier; he was jealous, perhaps unknowingly, of Laurier's eminence and achievement. It was a struggle between them as to who would go down in history as the authentic voice of French Canada.

Taft wants free trade

The last great issue loomed in 1910. A thousand westerners massed on Parliament Hill to complain of high prices caused by high tariffs. They were in Laurier's mind that fall when American President William Taft sent a team to Ottawa to sound him out on free trade. Taft's spokesmen were extraordinarily frank. American factories were overproducing; they had "wantonly exhausted" their resources; they needed Canada's raw materials and markets. In return they offered free or near-free access to theirs. In January 1911, the Laurier government announced that it had ne-

gotiated a draft reciprocity agreement with the Americans, the kind of low tariff agreement every Canadian government had been hoping to achieve since Confederation.

Critics across the country and the Conservative Party came out against reciprocity as the thin edge of a wedge leading to political union. Clifford Sifton, now completely in the enemy's camp, was their master strategist in the election campaign that autumn. Their "unholy" allies in Quebec were Bourassa's *nationalistes*, who denounced Laurier as a "traitor to his race" for his naval policy, which they magnified into impending conscription and press-gangs to drag French Canadians off to die for Britain.

Laurier loses in 1911

Shocked and hurt, Laurier spoke fifty times in a month, but it was too late. In Quebec he was the imperialist; in Ontario the annexationist. "I am neither," he cried in vain. "I am a Canadian. I have had before me ... a policy of true Canadianism, of moderation, of conciliation." In the federal election on September 21, 1911, Laurier lost almost all of Ontario and nearly half of Quebec.

He ended as he began, in opposition, reviled by World War I zealots, impaled on that cross of race. But he had staked his claim to greatness. He had been a dynamic leader, economically and politically. He had reshaped a Liberal party through which Quebec could rejoin Canada and shored up the foundations of national unity.

Some years later, after Laurier's death in 1919, his friend and sometime enemy, J. W. Dafoe of the *Manitoba Free Press*, would say:
He died the unquestioned leader, the idol of his people; and it may well be that as the centuries pass he will become the legendary embodiment of the race ... As for Bourassa, he may live in Canadian history ... by reason of his relations with the man he fought.

Election news hot off the press drew this Toronto crowd to the offices of the Evening Telegram *in 1908. Newspapers and word of mouth were the main sources of information in this era; radio news reports didn't begin until the 1930s. Newspaper circulation doubled during the decade, as Canada's population soared and cities grew larger.*

Cartoon Issues

Many up-to-date newspapers and magazines began running political cartoons in this decade. Although printing them was slow and expensive, competition from the U.S.A. and rising circulations prompted many publishers to go for the laughs and lampoons. These cartoonists were a gentler breed than their vitriolic 19th century cousins, who helped drive the Tories from power in the 1890s. Their scope ranged from great issues in Canadian-American relations (with Jack Canuck usually besting Uncle Sam) to the lighter side where a fearsome WCTU foursome could keep honourable members honest and readers laughing.

AUCTIONEER JOHNNY CANUCK. —Now, Gentlemen, make your bids, how much am I offered?

Auctioneer Johnny Canuck minds the merchandise while Uncle Sam and Britain's John Bull dominate the bidding for Canadian trade. Lesser customers look on.

F. D. MONK (soliloquizing)—If I can but give it life and shape once more, perchance 't will lead us to victory instead of grinning at us from the Party Cupboard.

Will Fred Monk, a prominent Quebec Conservative MP, revive the Manitoba School Question of the 1890s to use as ammunition against PM Laurier?

MAKING A CLEAN SWEEP.
What we may expect the ladies of the W.C.T.U. to accomplish, now that our law-makers have forsworn the cigarette.

Hatchet-faced, hatchet-toting temperance crusaders are the butt of this cartoon on the anti-smoking movement. The WCTU ladies' campaigns were not subtle.

32

Uncle Sam looks pretty suspicious as trainloads of his people head through Jack Canuck's wide-open border, but the caption assures us he's not too miffed, since they'll get "square treatment" in their new homeland. American immigrants were prized above others in the great land rush.

The American-Abell company's colourful 1904 calendar reminds customers that the maple leaf is forever. That was Regina's last year c/o the N.W.T.

"The sun never sets on the Canadian Airmotor," is the motto on the cover of this 1900 catalogue. "Wind engines" churned out farm power at the time.

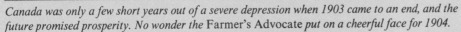

Canada was only a few short years out of a severe depression when 1903 came to an end, and the future promised prosperity. No wonder the Farmer's Advocate put on a cheerful face for 1904.

This ad hints that a National Cream Separator will not only modernize your farm, but will also keep your milk maid happy.

Enticing pamphlets like this one were churned out by the department of the interior in its energetic campaign to settle the Prairies. The government was especially keen to get Americans to move north because of their proven ability to farm the Prairies, but the call also went out to Eastern Europeans and Britons. Canada's population jumped from five to seven million in the short space of a decade.

The Last Best West

When Mrs. McNeil saw the sod house which was to be her home...she sat down and cried.

Reminiscences of Pioneer Life, Mary C. Bailey

"Free land!" Vassil Paish told the man in the sheepskin coat. "One hundred and sixty acres free. And only $15 a year in taxes. Just for the cost of getting to Hamburg, the steamship ticket, the train to Winnipeg. Seventy-five dollars, plus something for food and lodging."

Freedom, thought the man in the sheepskin coat. No payoffs to the local *pahn*, no church tithes, no army conscription. Freedom for the price of a pair of oxen. If I sell all that I own perhaps I can make it.

Thousands did. Throughout the Austro-Hungarian empire that year of 1901 scores of agents like Vassil Paish were persuading peasants to come to Canada. It was underground work; illegal. Even Paish did not know his employers: a group of European shipping lines working through the North Atlantic Trading Company. It was a clandestine network as secret as any espionage ring, and behind it, paying a bonus on every person channelled to Canada, was a young Canadian in Ottawa, Clifford Sifton.

Sifton had started in law in Brandon, Manitoba, earning, as he often said, only $428 a year. By 1896 he was rich from land speculation.

He knew the West; he had served five years as Manitoba's attorney general. Laurier had tapped him that year for his cabinet, as minister of the interior, with the job of filling the near-empty West. Sifton had been a thirty-five-year-old among eminent seniors then, a stony-faced, closed-mouthed man growing slowly deaf. By 1901 he was a cabinet powerhouse. He had sold the world on Canada, launching the last North American land rush, transforming a nation known in Britain five years before as "a slough of despond" into "the Cinderella of the western world."

The yearly increase in population when Sifton had tackled immigration was less than 1 per cent, the lowest in two centuries. After thirty years of settlement from Ontario, only about 400,000 people, one-quarter of them Indians, lived between the Great Lakes and the Rockies. As one newspaper exclaimed, "The trails from Manitoba to the States are worn bare and brown by the wagon wheels of departing settlers." The two best-read chapters of the Bible in the northwest, it was said, were *Lamentations* and *Exodus*.

So come to Alberta, there's room for you all,
Where the wind never ceases and the rain always
*   falls,*
Where the sun always sets and there it remains,
Till we get frozen out on our government claims.

Sifton pressured the railways to open 22.5 mil-

The CPR tried to lure Dutch settlers to the West with this poster, saying "The best crop and pasture land in the world" was waiting for them.

This immigrant ship in St. John brought few women: most newcomers in the era were single men. By 1911 Prairie men far outnumbered women. In Calgary, for example, there were 17,000 men to 9,000 women.

lion choice acres of land that they had been holding unused and untaxed. He restaffed his moribund department, cut away red tape and regulations, sent displays and booklets around the world and strung a web of agents across Europe. Into the great emigration funnel of Hamburg these agents herded their prospects: the peasants and labourers of eastern and northern Europe, the discontented, the adventurous, the oppressed. Sifton's shipping agents screened them, crammed them into the steerage of liners and disgorged them like cattle at Halifax and Quebec. In wooden cars equipped with cook-stoves they were shipped across the continent to be dumped out onto a flat, stoneless, near-treeless, slough-pitted prairie.

old-timers lasted a year

Those with money paid land-rush prices – up to $325 – for a wagon and horse. The others walked for days to reach their claims. They cut the sod and piled it to make a kind of earthen cave. They broke the soil with a single-furrow plough. And then the men walked back to town and took jobs laying train tracks to earn money for food, coal, tools, an axe, a gun, a proper house.

My house it is built of the natural soil,
My walls are erected according to Hoyle,
My roof has no pitch. It is level and plain,
And I always get wet when it happens to rain.

The women cooked jackrabbit day after day, hauled water from the slough and baked, enduring their loneliness; neighbours were often beyond the horizon. The men fought grasshopper plagues and grassfires started by train-engine sparks. In a winter storm the clothesline from house to shed was like a lifeline. An oldtimer was someone who lasted a year. It took back-breaking work, guts, faith and luck to survive.

This was wheat land and wheat was a gamble.

38

Sawflies could cut the crop like a scythe. Ice could fall like stones from the summer sky and flatten it. Drought could shrivel it, rust could blight it, frost could kill it. But a good crop, even cut with the wooden flail called a "poverty stick," could buy horses and machinery to work more land.

By 1901 the colonist cars had been running west for five years. Wars had been started for less land than Sifton was annually giving away. Yet the census returns were a shock. Canada had a mere 5,371,315 people, a gain of only a half-million in ten years. As fast as people were brought in, Sifton concluded, others left for the easier West to the south. "Never in the world's history, except in the case of Ireland," wrote O. D. Skelton, Laurier's biographer, "had there been such leakage of the brains and brawn of any country."

Sifton plugs the leak

Sifton set out to plug the leak, this time concentrating his efforts on the United States. He circulated millions of maps and illustrated brochures and dispatched lecturers to describe "the land of promise." He gave prosperous ex-Yankee wheat-growers free trips home to talk up Canada, took American writers joy-riding through "the largest continuous wheat field in the world." He advertised in 8,000 farm papers, and set up agents in eighteen cities. The American novelist Oliver Curwood, who worked for Sifton for two years, called it "a fight for people" carried on "with as much strategy and thought as though an actual war were being waged."

The inflow of Americans quickened. The Canadian settlers had clung to the rail line; the Americans headed for the North Saskatchewan River, where the rich humus of the Rockies covered the riverbanks for fifteen feet, and they forced the railway lines to come to them. They were men of means and know-how from Iowa and Nebraska,

farmers' sons who could not find land to buy at home, successful farmers who had sold out at a profit. They were making Alberta "a typical American state," Curwood noted later. "They do not regard themselves as aliens but as pioneers." They were buying land "in thousands of acres a day," warned the Toronto *World*, "and are preparing to control the factories and trade of the whole region." "The American invasion," imperialist newspapers called it. "The American peril."

Sifton turned this imperial sentiment to advantage. He brought over British writers to view the "invasion" and soon articles were appearing in the tenor of the *Fortnightly Review,* which cautioned, "We must not sit back any longer and watch one of the most promising daughter lands being peopled by settlers of alien blood."

Sifton gave many British villagers their first look at a car, incidentally displaying samples of wheat from the Eden on the frontier. He mailed maps free to British school children, offered prizes for essays on Canada. In 1900 less than 10,000 Britons a year had been leaving for Canada while the United States was getting three times as many. By 1904 emigration to Canada had soared to 50,000. By 1905, for the first time in fifty years, Canada was outdrawing the United States. And why not, when the Yanks themselves preferred it?

"No Englishmen need apply"

The Northwest became the testing ground of the English "remittance man," the younger and wilder sons of the English aristocracy, who lived on money remitted from home. Many were so unused to work that employment ads sometimes carried the postscript: "No Englishman need apply." Jimmy Simpson, a celebrated Rocky Mountain trailblazer, remembered:

Wherever you went at the turn of the century, you

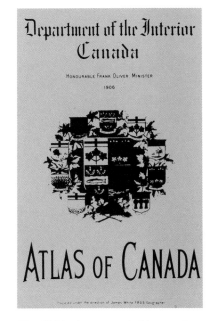

This 1906 atlas was probably out of date as soon as it came off the press. The face of the West was constantly changed by new settlers, new towns and railways pushing into new territory.

The Newcomers

The Prairie settlers were not pioneers in the sense of an earlier Canadian era. They were not self-sufficient: they fully expected to share the advantages of an industrial age, buying rather than making their own clothing, furniture and food. Their primitive sod or log houses were always considered temporary, and often were soon replaced by frame houses made with Ontario or British Columbia lumber. However, like early pioneers, they had to endure the cold, heat, insects, isolation and sometimes the hostility of neighbours who resented their language and customs.

Homesteaders like these, near Edmonton, stayed alive for the first two years through subsistence farming.

No "women's work" here. The Ruthenians shared most jobs.

Doukhobor women voluntarily pulled the plough when draught horses were not available for the job.

The Barr colonists erected a tent city in Saskatoon before their 200-mile trek to Battleford and beyond. Poor leadership almost destroyed their early attempts to settle.

"A stalwart peasant in the sheep-skin coat . . . and half-a-dozen children" was Clifford Sifton's idea of a valuable immigrant. These Galicians appear to fit the bill.

Settlers in the West were granted a quarter section of free land, provided they lived on it and farmed it for three years. This immigrant waited all night outside the Saskatoon land office to secure his free 160 choice acres.

Rich farmers could put steam power to work for them in the form of these giant tractors, some weighting 20 tons and capable of pulling a 14-furrow plough. When they weren't carving up the prairie the tractors powered threshing machines.

found some damfool Englishman looking for the outer rim of beyond the beyond. I remember four Englishmen digging a ditch for the government in Banff. They used to talk to each other in Latin. The foreman thought they were plotting against the government.

Bert Herridge, the British-born MP for Kootenay West, was eleven years old in 1906 when his family reached the Columbia Valley:

When we unloaded our belongings, my father turned to my mother and, pointing to the leather case containing his silk hat, said: "Charlotte, behold the symbol of the secure and certain past." He then pointed to a cross-cut saw we had picked up in Winnipeg and said: "And behold here the symbol of a damned uncertain future!"

The British planted fruit trees in the valleys of British Columbia, stocked the rangeland of southern Alberta with purebred cattle and Arabian horses. Mormons from Utah built canals through the dust bowl near Lethbridge, beginning a great irrigation project and Alberta's sugar beet industry. The Dutch began strip farming and the Chinese opened restaurants. The plains were dotted with place-names that told of their founders' origins: Tolstoi, Prague, Rosthern, Viking, Humboldt, Ukrainia, Edam. There were more foreign-language newspapers there than anywhere in the world. The west was now one of the strangest places on earth, where Hutterites practised communism and Doukhobors sometimes refused to wear clothes. A place where, as a St. Paul paper put it, "you can leave home after Easter, sow your grain and take in your harvest, and come home with your pockets full . . . for Thanksgiving dinner."

42

By the decade's end some settlers were becoming wealthy. W.T. "Horseshoe" Smith was preparing to build the largest barn in the world – longer than a football field and six storeys high – for his huge Saskatchewan alfalfa and corn farm.

Peter Verigin
Czar of the Doukhobors

The reality was seldom like that, but that was the popular view. Europe's growing cities needed bread, and wheat was a magic word. The Canadian government tried to interest homesteaders in mixed farming. "Then a good wheat crop would come along and everybody would go crazy," said Dr. J. G. Rutherford, then Canada's veterinary director general. "They would shut the cheese factories and let the cattle freeze." An exaggeration perhaps, but only in emphasis. The new westerner was a businessman who produced one product for cash, not a subsistence farmer who grew his own food.

Like all regions in ferment, the West was now a land of contrasts. At the same time that U.S. *Technical World* proclaimed: "Canada teems with wealth," a mounted policeman entered a snow-covered cabin from which no smoke was rising and found a family of ten huddled together without

fuel or food, trying to keep each other warm while they starved. While steam-powered tractors lumbered across the plains like latter-day mammoths, teams of Doukhobor women hitched themselves like horses to the ploughs.

Here, for a sweep of a thousand miles, was a flatland made for machinery, weathered by centuries into a clay loam, protected in winter by snow. The summer sun shone hot and long. The nights were cool and the rains were light, so that the protein-building nitrates remained in the soil. It was, as a Minnesota miller said, "the finest wheat area in the world."

At the 1904 St. Louis World's Fair, Canadian spring and fall wheat won gold medals. "Manitoba No. 1 Northern" was now a synonym for top quality. It earned $50 million that year and Agriculture Minister Sydney Fisher claimed that it gave his farmers an income "40 per cent greater than the

When Peter Verigin stepped off the train at Winnipeg in 1903, it was obvious he was not one of the immigrants in sheepskin coats. He was tall, handsome, articulate and impeccably dressed. The *Free Press* called him "Kingly." After years in Siberian exile, he was joining his people, the Russian religious sect, the Doukhobors, who had come to Canada four years earlier. Verigin was the man the Doukhobors needed: their community of 7,500 was plagued by economic and political problems. Within a year of Verigin's arrival, they had bought $114,000 in land and farm equipment, and under his strict leadership became almost self-sufficient, both in Saskatchewan and in a B.C. colony founded in 1908. Self-taught, mystical, autocratic and shrewd, he remained their "czar" until 1924 when he was killed by a time bomb planted in his train car. The assassin was never found.

Cora Hind
The Wizard of Grain

"Extraordinary that a woman could predict the size of a prairie wheat crop!" said one newspaper, but Cora Hind could and did. Born in 1861, and an orphan, she moved from Ontario with her aunt to Winnipeg at age 21. There she applied for a job at the *Free Press* but was turned down because she was a woman. But Cora Hind wasn't easily discouraged. She rented a typewriter, one of the first available on the market, learned to use it and set up business as the first woman public stenographer in the West. The *Free Press* agreed to hire her in 1901, and she quickly took over the agricultural editor's desk. In that post she became known as a world-wide authority on grain, livestock and dairy conditions and prices. Active even in her later years, at 74 she visited 27 countries on an agricultural fact-finding tour, and worked until her death in 1942 in the WCTU's campaign for women's rights.

average income of farmers in the United States." Canada had been founded on furs and lumber; now it had a third staple, easy to ship and in world-wide demand. And, like all great staples, wheat was transforming the country that produced it.

Railways were needed to transport wheat, and tracks were piercing the wheatland at an average clip of two miles a day. As fast as stations went up, elevators to store the wheat rose beside them, and young clerks got off the trains with a thousand dollars pinned inside their coats to set up bank branches. When the railway went through North Battleford land was $6 an acre; six months later it was $10 a foot. "There isn't a tinhorn gambler left in Nevada," an American journalist wrote. "They are all selling town lots in Canada!"

Winnipeg was the tollgate

One visiting journalist described his western trip with some railway surveyors. They stopped and brought out their surveying instruments:

to determine on the map the exact spot. "We will put a town here," said the engineer in charge. The man who held the map put a spot on his sheet. Other men made marks on the ground . . . The party got into their wagons and drove on for perhaps another ten miles to assist at the birth of another town just like the first.

Winnipeg was financier and tollgate to the prairies, a boom-town of 65,000 in 1904. Its bordellos and saloons were as busy as merchants like Jimmy Ashdown, who parlayed a tinker's solder stick into Canada's biggest hardware store. The city had hundreds of real estate agents; so many "vacant lots" ringed its outskirts that the city council had to go five miles out for parkland.

Winnipeg's railway yards were, by 1904, the largest in the world, with as many as 1,800 freight cars passing through in a single fall day. The world's largest grain elevators were rising at the Lakehead. Huge grain carriers were being built in the shipyards of the St. Lawrence to float the harvest through canals deepened in 1903 to fourteen feet. The wheat was in the heart of a continent and it fathered a transport system unrivalled for speed and efficiency.

In 1905 20 per cent more prairie sod was broken and 146,000 more immigrants poured into Canada. Each newcomer, each new town called for products, goods and services. Regina was now the distributing point for hundreds of implement agencies. Drummers peddled churns, treadle sewing machines, foot-pumped organs. At Leader, Saskatchewan, W. T. "Horseshoe" Smith built "the world's largest barn," using 30,000 sacks of cement and 875,000 board feet of lumber.

Like a blood transfusion the money from wheat energized the entire economy. Factories in eastern Canada doubled their plant space. Steel production jumped in a decade from 20,000 to 82,-000 tons a year. Fall unemployment vanished as the railways coupled their oldest cars in "Harvester's Specials" that carried an army of easterners west to man the threshers for the highest casual pay east of British Columbia: $2 a day.

the top wheat exporter

From 18 million bushels a year in 1896, the wheat yield would rise in 1911 to over 78 million. After the bitter dispute with Laurier over separate schools, Sifton resigned in 1905 amid rumours that he had made millions in insider deals in land. He had done his job so well that his successor, Frank Oliver, was given Canada's first million-dollar advertising budget.

Canada was now the world's leading exporter of wheat. Bankers in foreign cities studied reports by Cora Hind, *Manitoba Free Press* reporter and prophetess of the wheat belt. "Everywhere the talk is of the west, 'Are you going west? Have you been west?'" wrote Dr. Arthur Shadwell in the London *Times* in 1907. "In Europe more is heard of that than of anything else."

The boom paused briefly in 1909. "There is no crop whatever in the southern part of Manitoba, Saskatchewan and Alberta – everything has been devoured by intense heat and drought," Laurier reported that year from Somerset, Manitoba, to Lord Grey, the man who had replaced Lord Minto as governor general in 1904. But drought didn't stop the settlers. "Far from it," wrote Laurier, "they are as buoyant as ever and say this is part of the game."

They pushed into Peace River country and along the upper Fraser, they fenced the bunch-grass valleys of the Nechako. They came from as far away as Japan, India and Patagonia.

It was the last and greatest of the North American migrations. By the time it was over Canada's wheat crop had been increased to ten times its size in 1900. The "last, best west" on the last western continent had been reached.

Immigration was the most impressive achievement of the decade and, though many would have come to the prairies anyway, much credit goes to Sifton, the finest press agent of his time. In 1900 the world knew Canada only through the CPR, the Mounties and the Klondike. Within a few years the lure of free land made it the fastest growing country in the world, with a population growth rate for the decade of more than 34 per cent. He had given away a kingdom in land to gain two million people, more than tripling the population of the prairies. He had helped create two new provinces and made the West one of the greatest granaries in the world.

Wheat financed the modern nation and immigrants grew the wheat. It was the immigrants, most of them poor, who made the country rich. It was these aliens who gave us a national economy.

A farmer's only hope against a raging barn fire was a cloudburst: on the dry prairies, that left little hope indeed. Fire departments were miles away and water was usually scarce, so destruction was total, as in this Manitoba fire.

Grand Hotels

It was the age of wealth and optimism, a time of fortunes made and fortunes spent. In fits of extravagance railway magnates erected stately hotels in all the major cities–Quebec's Chateau Frontenac, Toronto's King Edward, the Hotel Vancouver and Victoria's Empress, among others shown on these postcards. This was luxury the country had never seen before–imported marble, Irish linen, gold and silver-plated dinnerware and fine china. Just the sort of place for million-aires to clink glasses of brandy (Napoleon, of course) and speak of mergers. As early as 1910 the King Edward was the rallying-point for Toronto's high-rollers. The interiors were grandly *art nouveau*–great sweeping mahogany bannisters held up with gracious loops and whorls of brass and wrought iron, fashioned after the most exotic vegetation. Chandeliers–but of course! Tourists and travelling businessmen could bask in continental opulence. Those were the days of real elegance!

Algonquin Hotel, St. Andrews, N.B.

Vancouver Hotel, Vancouver, B.C.

KING EDWARD HOTEL, TORONTO.

View of Broadway, Winnipeg, Canada
Showing the "Fort Garry," The Grand Trunk Pacific
$2,000,000 Hotel and The Union Station

The New Windsor Hotel. MONTREAL.

Chateau Frontenac from Laval University, Quebec. On line of C.P.R.

Rotunda, Prince George Hotel
Toronto, Canada.

Grand Hotel, Yarmouth, N.S.

C.P.R. Hotel "Empress," Victoria, B.C

The enormous steam locomotive on the right dwarfs even the tallest of these workers on the Canadian Northern Railway. In 1896 William Mackenzie and Donald Mann purchased the Lake Manitoba Railway, the first in a long series of acquisitions which in the next decade and a half they tied together into Canada's second trans-continental railway.

CHAPTER FOUR

What! Another Railway?

Canada's great artists today are . . . writing a new kind of blank verse in town sites and railway iron and grain routes.

The Globe

"In these days of wonderful development," Laurier told the House in 1903, it is "our duty, immediate and imperative," to build a second transcontinental railway. With this decision he triggered Canada's biggest spending spree and opened the last and longest of the three heydays of railroading, during which two Ontario farmboys pulled off the century's boldest promotion – a prodigy of private enterprise that pushed a reluctant nation into a vast adventure in public ownership.

William Mackenzie and Donald Mann had teamed up in 1896, two contractors with a charter to build a rail line northwest of Winnipeg. The line had been only a hundred miles "from nowhere to nowhere," as one writer said, and it took only thirteen men and a boy to run it. In five years it was Canada's third-largest railroad. And Mackenzie, the one-time storekeeper, and Mann, the former lumber-camp foreman, were no longer contractors on the make but railway moguls – in a day when a railway president in his top hat and private car was the closest thing in Canada to a duke.

The CPR, the world's largest railway system, was by then almost a law unto itself. Manitoba had brought in the American Northern Pacific to break the monopoly, but the rates had somehow stayed disappointingly high. Manitobans hated railway monopolies, and Mackenzie and Mann built their first little line into Winnipeg by manipulating emotion rather than money.

Mackenzie, then forty-nine, and Mann, forty-six, bought 3,000 bushels of seed grain and gave it to settlers on their line. "Service was our motto," said Dave Hanna, their general manager, in the insider's account he wrote thirty years later. "We had more stopping places to the ten miles, I think, than any railway in the world." Trains would stop to deliver a hind of beef or an invitation to supper.

The settlers responded with almost pathetic gratitude. They loaded freight and repaired the tracks without pay, as if the railway had been a community project. The politicians were pleased, both in Winnipeg and Ottawa, though Laurier did not entirely approve of Mackenzie and Mann.

In 1901 the grateful Manitoba government sublet more than 300 miles of Northern Pacific branch lines it had taken over to Mackenzie and Mann. They had been buying and building track running in every direction, and now their whole system, consolidated as the Canadian Northern, was the CPR's chief western rival, covering 1,200 miles from the Lakehead to Saskatchewan.

In 1901 6.5 million bushels of Canada's grain had gone over the Northern Pacific to the American port of Duluth; in 1902 the grain went over

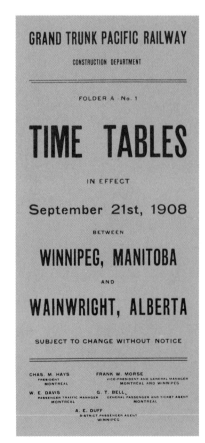

The GTP timetable could not schedule the financial ruin around the next bend. Business shrank, debts piled up, and the government took over in 1919.

Mr. Mackenzie and Mr. Mann

William MacKenzie was the financial wizard in the partnership, successfully badgering governments for a total of a quarter-billion dollars to pour into the railway.

Donald Mann was also adept at getting subsidies from politicians, and his long experience in railways helped him keep construction moving at a tremendous pace.

THE GROWING TIME FOR TRANS-CONTINENTAL RAILWAYS.

The Premier : "The People pay for and give you the Railways, and make you a present of the country ;—but what do they get as a quid pro quo?"
Chorus : "The People—as represented by the Government—will get–er–our vote and influence, you know."

the Canadian Northern to Port Arthur. And the line was making money: better than $600,000 a year. Mackenzie and Mann now cut their freight rates by 15 per cent.

A howl of anguish went up from the CPR chairman, William Van Horne, but Mann and Mackenzie were heroes on the prairies. Prosperity followed wherever they built; new communities clamoured for new lines. The West was swept with an optimism that quickened even the cautious. "Within four or five years," said Edmund Walker, general manager of the Canadian Bank of Commerce, after his first trip west in 1902, "every railroad in the country will have to double-track its lines." Mackenzie and Mann's sensational success made railways the talk of the times, the base and symbol of national growth, the cause and effect of prosperity. And in this atmosphere Charles M. Hays, general manager of the Grand Trunk, announced a second transcontinental railway.

coast-to-coast prestige

Laurier was delighted. The Grand Trunk had prestige. A coast-to-coast line would be his monument, as the CPR had been Sir John A.'s. It would satisfy Sifton, who hated to see prairie wheat fattening ports in the United States. It would please the Maritimes, suffering because the CPR and the Grand Trunk were emptying Canadian produce into American east-coast terminals. It would open the farm and timber lands of northern Quebec and Ontario and win him support from the colonizing Catholic Church. Besides, the nation could not grow on the single wheat-choked CPR line.

But Laurier soon learned that Hays had lukewarm support from his London directors. The president, Sir Charles Rivers Wilson, had met Mackenzie and was impressed. The Canadian Northern served the West; the Grand Trunk served the East, 3,000 miles stretching west as far as Sudbury. Competition was folly, Wilson felt, but a merger – that made sense. He repeatedly urged it on Hays and Laurier.

Hays, dynamic, conniving and autocratic, ignored him. An American, he dreamed of emulating the one-time American telegraphist Van Horne, who had won such wealth and history-book fame in Canada. At Laurier's request Hays met twice with Mann and Mackenzie. But he was unfriendly, Mann testified later:

We offered to build a joint section from North Bay to Port Arthur.... We would develop the west and they would develop the east.... They refused and would not do anything but buy us out. We were too young and ambitious to sell out at that time.

Laurier wanted the Grand Trunk transcontinental; Hays wanted it; between them they coerced Wilson. The Speech from the Throne in March 1903 announced the great joint venture: the government would build the eastern half from Moncton to Winnipeg; the Grand Trunk (Pacific) would build from Winnipeg to Prince Rupert.

split the cabinet

The issue split the cabinet. It was "premature," Sifton said. "Ill-conceived and of dubious national advantage." Always the strong man, Sifton would have told Hays and Mackenzie to merge, or else. Andrew Blair, the minister of railways, resigned from the cabinet; Laurier, usually correct and courteous, had not brought Blair into his railway discussions, perhaps because Blair was close to Mann and Mackenzie. In the House, as in the cabinet, debates were heated. But only Robert Borden, the Opposition leader, came up with a sensible suggestion: public ownership and joint use of the CPR line through the trafficless wilderness. "The $200 million vote-catcher," the Tories called Laurier's line. "Designed to carry elections rather

than passengers."

During the following 1904 election campaign distraught friends came to Laurier with rumours of a cloak-and-dagger plot. The disgruntled Blair and his friend Dave Russell, who owned the Saint John *Telegraph* and the *Evening Times*, had joined forces with Hugh Graham, the Tory who owned the *Montreal Star*. They had put up $1 million to buy *La Presse*, Laurier's Montreal mouthpiece. Although code names and passwords were used in the secret midnight negotiations, the buyers were thought to include an accountant and a lawyer for Mann and Mackenzie. They would use *La Presse*, it was said, to reveal a series of Liberal scandals, defeat Laurier, and kill the Grand Trunk project.

grid-iron the prairies

Laurier acted. He talked privately to Blair, presumably the source of information on the scandals, and none broke. Laurier won his election and cabled Wilson: "Our victory is so complete as to leave no doubt that our railway policy is extremely popular. The opposition made a grave mistake in adopting a policy of government ownership and operation."

In a rare interview Mackenzie made his disappointment clear. "You know we expected at one time to be the favourite people to build this transcontinental road. Now we must get along as best we can." But their strategy was unchanged: to grid-iron the prairies, make friends while they built and consolidate a political base for expansion.

Gambling that farmers would brave frost for black soil, they thrust tracks into the Northwest. Their sheaf of old charters gave them more than four million acres of land and if the traffic was not there they created it, selling land on credit. "As long as a man is on his farm and is improving his property for the railroad either in the shape of

Hugh Graham
The Press Baron of Montreal

The chief election issue in the 1904 campaign was railways, and behind closed doors in Montreal a plot was hatched to undermine Laurier's Grand Trunk and throw support to Mackenzie and Mann's Canadian Northern project. In the thick of the intrigue was the *Star*'s founder and publisher, Hugh Graham, the ex-newsboy who controlled the country's largest-circulation English-language daily. He had founded the *Star* in 1869 at age 21, and had often used its pages to fight his personal battles. Now he was involved in a scheme to buy the Quebec daily, *La Presse*, and use its influence to discredit and scandalize the Liberals out of office. The plot failed, and Laurier won the election. Graham's vitriolic editorials and pro-British views got him into trouble during WW I, and in 1917 his mansion near Montreal was dynamited by terrorists plotting to force repeal of conscription. He died in Montreal in 1938, after seventy years in journalism.

**Max Aitken
Our Lord Beaverbrook**

The new century, prosperity, new technology and a new business ethic ushered in the corporation era, and no one understood the business of mergers better than New Brunswick's Max Aitken. Born in 1879, the son of a minister, he published his first newspaper under the motto "We lead, let those follow who can." He never looked back. At 26 he was already director of Royal Securities Corp. and financial advisor to bankers and investors. Before he was 30, he negotiated the $100 million merger of three of the biggest companies in Canada. But he showed little more than initial interest in the corporations. "I am a builder," he said. From 1910-1945 he headed several ministries in the British government, put together one of the largest news empires in the world, and until his death in 1964 was a supporter of universities and the arts in Canada.

grain or of cattle," Hanna said, "we do not do anything to force him to make payment."

In 1905, building on government-backed bonds, they reached Edmonton, creating more than a hundred towns as they went. Mann was the hefty, hard-driving, brash and exuberant construction boss. He generated such enthusiasm, Hanna said, that employees would "work all through the night, take time out for a morning shave and breakfast and continue uninterruptedly for another day." Mackenzie was the moneyman, thickset, handsome, intense, self-contained.

hodgepodge of lines

Behind them was an extraordinary team: Hanna; the legendary lobbyist Billy Moore; the corporation lawyer Zebulon Lash whose mind, Hanna said, had "the exactitude of a multiplication table and the clarity of a mirror," and the most successful fund-raiser in Britain, Robert Horne-Payne. It was later claimed at a royal commission that British funds raised by Horne-Payne for Canada totalled $250 million – one-quarter of Britain's pre-World-War-I investment in the Dominion – and that of this, four-fifths was for the Canadian Northern.

By 1909 Mackenzie and Mann were handling one-third of the prairie grain traffic. They had bought or built a hodgepodge of lines in Ontario, Quebec and Nova Scotia. They were building from Toronto to Sudbury; they would build anywhere, it seemed. With a straight face, Mann once assured one interviewer that construction to the Yukon would start as soon as his engineers had found a method of tunnelling through glaciers.

The Canadian Northern was setting a pace that its rivals could not ignore. In 1905 the CPR earmarked $100 million for feeder lines in Ontario and the prairies. It put two thousand men to work cutting grades in the tunnels of Kicking Horse

Pass, the most contorted railway track on the continent. It undertook on Vancouver Island what one writer called at the time "the largest land-clearing contract in Western America." Always the visionary, CPR chairman Sir William Van Horne saw his system stretching from Euston, England, to Hong Kong and Sydney, Australia.

Nor was Charles Hays to be outdone. He spent $50 million for the finest road on the prairies, put up 131 grain elevators and constructed three hotels – the Macdonald Hotel in Edmonton, the Fort Garry in Winnipeg, and the Chateau Laurier in Ottawa. He surrounded himself with Americans as tough and highhanded as he was and expended goodwill as recklessly as he spent his shareholders' money. He embittered labour by trying to break his railway union. He alienated British Columbia by trying to import Chinese labour. He ignored the needs of communities in locating his lines in Saskatchewan. He crossed eighty highways without permission in Alberta. In one case the head of the Board of Railway Commissioners called the conduct of the Grand Trunk Pacific: "Grossest deceit . . . a breach of faith of the worst character. . . . If a private individual had done what this company had done he would probably land in the penitentiary." But the Grand Trunk, the owner of Hays' Grand Trunk Pacific, was the biggest corporation in Canada next to the CPR.

government spending

Of them all, however, the biggest spender was the government. Its portion of the new transcontinental crossed the St. Lawrence at Quebec City with the world's highest single-span bridge, which twice collapsed, killing eighty-five men. The road threaded the Shield for nearly half its 1,800 miles and cost close to a quarter-billion dollars. It was called by the New York *Herald* "the largest single enterprise . . . by any railway interest in America," and by Laurier's biographer, O. D. Skelton, "the most corrupting single factor since Confederation." It was a Liberal grab-bag. Insiders bought up and priced up its right-of-way. Contracts were padded; loose rock was classified as solid rock, tripling payment. It cost twice as much and took twice as long to build as it should have. (It was not to be in service till June 1915.)

In the meantime Mackenzie and Mann went on peddling their government-backed bonds. Mackenzie, it was reported, had a second headquarters in Ottawa and a branch office in every provincial capital except Prince Edward Island. When Canadian Northern lobbyists entered Laurier's office, the prime minister would ask, "Well, what does Mr. Mackenzie want now?"

hailed as demigods

By the decade's end they had linked Quebec, Ottawa and Montreal. They were reaching into Alberta coal country, Athabasca fur country, Peace River cattle country, the Sudbury mining area. They operated coal and iron mines, gypsum and copper mines; Mann, it was said, would grubstake anyone who showed him an ore sample. They ran two Atlantic steamships, a ferry to Vancouver Island, express and telegraph companies, whale and halibut fisheries, grain elevators, lumber mills and three luxury hotels. A chart of their incorporations, Hanna said, would resemble the family tree of the kings of England.

Mackenzie and Mann were the men of the hour. Reporters hung on their words, hailed them as demigods and wonder-workers. People would stop in the street and say, "Isn't that William Mackenzie? They say this time he's brought back sixty million dollars from Threadneedle Street." They were considered the greatest industrial builders of the age. "I never was a William Mackenzie," Max Aitken, later Lord Beaverbrook, said just

The Quebec Bridge collapse of 1907, which killed seventy-five workers, was blamed on an "error in judgement" by the engineers. Ten more died in a second collapse before the bridge was completed in 1917.

The Grand Trunk Pacific (later CNR) station at Yorkton, Sask. When the CPR built through here in 1890 it missed the townsite by three miles – so the town moved.

after he put together the Steel Company of Canada. "I created nothing as he did."

By decade's end the wave of incoming capital was cresting. Within two years it would slacken, and war would end it. But the forces set in motion could not be stopped. Carried on by their own momentum, by ambition, by competition, Mackenzie and Mann and Hays and the government went on building and spending to give Canada, by 1915, three transcontinental railways, a duplication so costly that Laurier's successor, Robert Borden, called the mounting burden of bond interest "a nightmare" and set up a royal commission to investigate.

The commission found that Mackenzie and Mann had built fast and well. They had watered their stock but their prairie roads had always paid their way. All but 10 per cent of the people on the prairies were on their lines. They had acted as a kind of public works project that gave many set-tlers their first stake. They had not only ridden the boom, they had helped create it. They had staged a great pageant of finance: they had built a railroad of ten thousand miles – three times as long as the first CPR line – an epic of audacity. But in doing it they had overbuilt and overcapitalized Canada. They had doomed the railways to be perennial pensioners. They were guilty, as the commission said, of "unreasoning optimism."

The optimism ended in catastrophe. Economic despression ruined business and scuttled the Grand Trunk, weakening Canada's credit in Britain for years. Laurier had let events decide policy, let greed and ambition run rampant, let his transcontinental monument become a monumental problem that no railway commission has yet been able to solve. But then, as O. D. Skelton pointed out: "Bankers, manufacturers, merchants, western farmers, inventors and speculators from end to end of the country shared the same fever."

Steam Railway Mileage.	
Alberta Ry. and Irrigation Co.	111.82
Albert Southern	19.00
Algoma Central and Hudson's Bay	89.64
Atlantic and Lake Superior	100.00
Atlantic, Quebec and Western	......
Bay of Quinte	89.37
Bedlington and Nelson	23.97
Beersville Coal and Ry. Co.	8.63
British Yukon	90.32
Brockville, Westport and North-Western	45.00
Bruce Mines and Algoma	17.28
Buctouche and Moncton	32.00
Brandon, Saskatchewan and Hudson's Bay	69.45
Bessemer and Barry's Bay	5.00
Canada Coals and Ry. Co.	12.00
Canada Southern	382.19
Canada Government Railways—	
Intercolonial	1,451.19
Prince Edward Island	267.50
Canadian Northern	2,584.50
Canadian Northern Ontario	146.80
Canadian Northern Quebec	251.60
Canadian Pacific	8,883.30
Cape Breton	31.00
Caraquet	84.78
Carillon and Grenville	13.00
Central Ontario	136.49
Crow's Nest Southern	53.20
Cumberland Ry. and Coal Co.	32.00
Dominion Atlantic	277.96
Edmonton, Yukon and Pacific	4.50
Elgin and Havelock	28.00

By March 1908, exactly 22,451.71 miles of track had been woven across the dominion: quite a jump from 1836, when Canada's first iron horse set out along the 14½ miles of wooden rail run by the Champlain and St. Lawrence Railway.

Every spike these navvies drove into the GTP line further sealed the company's fate: ruin through over-extension.

CHAPTER FIVE

Prof. Tory and the "Knitwits"

*If I were founding a university – and I say
it with all the seriousness of which I am
capable – I would found first a smoking room.*

Stephen Leacock

In the fall of 1904 a Vancouver teacher, Lemuel Robertson, came back to Montreal for postgraduate work at McGill University obsessed by what most of his colleagues considered an impossible idea: that the time was ripe for a university in British Columbia.

Canada had seventeen universities, but none west of Winnipeg, and only students from wealthy families could afford the long trip east. An attempt in 1890 to set up a university on the west coast had failed because of jealousy between Vancouver and Victoria. Robertson stressed the need to all whom he thought might help, among them Henry Marshall (Marsh) Tory, a McGill mathematics professor.

It was a lucky meeting of minds. Marsh Tory had grown up on his family's Nova Scotia farm, fishing, hunting and reading borrowed books. Learning that Cardinal Wolsey had his BA from Oxford at the age of fourteen inspired him to try to go to college and be a preacher. At twenty-two, after five years of clerking and teaching, studying at night, he had saved $200, enough for one term at McGill. By cramming and skimping on sleep he won the scholarships he needed and went on to get an MA, the Anne Molson Medal and a DSc. Then

he took a job teaching math at McGill while he studied for the ministry. By the time he was ordained, however, he was deeply involved in teaching.

He had now been fifteen years at McGill, "a striking, distinguished looking man, about five foot ten, stockily built," his biographer, E.A. Corbett, described him. He gave an "impression of intense intellectual and physical energy." His trim triangular moustache gave him a look of sternness, but that was belied by the "perpetual twinkle" of his eyes.

Tory at that time was urging McGill to help – by affiliation – small, struggling colleges outside Quebec. McGill was privately endowed, free of church and political control. It had already affiliated with five small Quebec colleges. Tory's campaign had won affiliation that year for three colleges in the Maritimes – Acadia, Mount Allison and King's. He was a man looking for a cause and now along came Lemuel Robertson with his plan for turning Vancouver High School into Vancouver College. Tory talked it up and sold the idea to McGill's principal, William Peterson.

Peterson sent Tory west in the spring of 1905. Within a few weeks he reported that he had:

talked school and college matters with every man in British Columbia whose knowledge would help me to gauge opinion . . .

The greatest difficulty, he found, was:

"McGill Men"

are noted for their good taste in the matter of dress. It is a well known fact that many of the best dressed men at "Old McGill" wear FIT-REFORM Suits and Overcoats.

MONTREAL WARDROBE
444 St. Catherine St. W.

According to this ad McGill men were known for more than their brains. The natural shoulder came into vogue at the end of the decade – fit reform.

Opposite page: *School and church (Anglican) officials crowd the steps for the King's College encaenia (graduation) in N.S. Most universities were still religiously affiliated.*

Henry "Marsh" Tory (left) poses with his brothers each sporting a unique moustache. In his career Tory guided universities across Canada and the "Khaki University" in England after WW I.

the local jealousies. . . . If the government gives consent to one High School to extend its affiliation it cannot refuse it to another. . . . They have only a majority of three in the House and deciding on a place for a university might mean defeat.

To get itself off the hook, the government asked Tory to decide the location. He chose Vancouver and worked out a plan to offer two years in arts and sciences. The college should be a corporation, he said, to attract funds. University graduates in British Columbia would have a substantial voice in its administration.

site by the sea

The government was so pleased with his plan they donated a magnificent seaside site. The Vancouver School Board agreed to help pay for buildings, scientific equipment, and four teachers' salaries at $460 a year each. Tory left for home in high spirits, stopping off at Calgary and Edmonton, where he called on the premier, Dr. A.C. Rutherford, who was also Alberta's minister of education.

All over Alberta, Rutherford said, towns were mushrooming. In the previous year 270 new school districts had been formed. Tory was fascinated. If McGill succeeded in British Columbia, it could open the field throughout the West.

Back in Montreal Tory's report was approved by the faculty of arts, by the corporation and by Peterson – only to be shelved by the board of governors.

The board was chaired and dominated by a diminutive Maritime Scot, Sir William Macdonald, an odd paradoxical character. His W.C. Macdonald Company was Canada's largest tobacco firm but he loathed the tobacco habit in any form. He was enormously wealthy yet he saved string and wrapping paper, and slept, according to his doctor, in an old iron bed in a small third-floor room of his mansion adjoining the campus. He had only a few years' schooling, yet he had given more to education than any man before or since in Canada.

McGill had struggled since 1813 – when fur trader James McGill's will gave it birth – until two students who didn't know any better had canvassed Macdonald for funds. The tight-fisted bachelor had unexpectedly taken McGill to his heart: extended the campus, built colleges, endowed chairs, set up scholarships. He had poured $13 million into McGill to make it a great university, but his princely giving was curiously streaked with stinginess. The year before, a thousand-dollar raise would have kept Dr. Robert McKenzie, the world's leading physical educationist and an eminent sculptor, from leaving McGill for the University of Pennsylvania. But Macdonald had refused it. "Professors," he had said, "will be giving dinner parties if they get such high salaries." Principal Peterson, his next-door neighbour and closest friend, had appealed to him personally for a grant to British Columbia, but in vain.

"Could I see him?" Tory asked.

he hated clergymen

Peterson was dubious. Tory was a minister and Sir William hated clergymen. His feelings were so deep that he wanted the university YMCA to drop the word McGill from its name. He supported education as a means of freeing people from what he called religious superstition. "It wouldn't do any good," Peterson said.

"It can't do any harm," Tory insisted. And Peterson reluctantly set up an interview.

Macdonald's office was in an old building on Notre Dame Street, a twelve-by-twelve-foot room with a dour Scot sitting outside to bar visitors. Sir William was perched on a kitchen chair behind a bare board table, his short body draped in a broadcloth frockcoat turning green with age. He had a sharp, lined face, sharp nose, sharp eyes. His greeting was cool.

Tory explained that British Columbia was in danger of repeating the mistakes of Nova Scotia, where no one college was doing first-rate research or first-rate teaching. Unless McGill helped the province set up a strong state-supported university, a number of weak church-supported schools like Columbian would spring up. Columbian was a Methodist college in New Westminster, affiliated with the University of Toronto. "Its ambitions," Tory said, "are beyond its strength. A strong step, taken now, would probably settle this question for all time, not only by making such institutions unnecessary but by making competition impossible." The sum needed was trifling: $5,000.

no sum was trifling

Tory had sparked his interest, but no sum was trifling to Sir William.

"I'll pledge you, Sir William, that if you'll supply the amount I have suggested for three years you will not be asked for another cent during that period. And further, if you will allow me to report progress from time to time, I promise you not to ask for money without first writing you for an interview. You may then refuse to discuss it without embarrassment."

Sir William no doubt realized that in pledging him no embarrassment Tory was shrewdly opening the door for more money. Nevertheless he agreed. "Under a cold exterior," Tory noted in his diary, he was "warm hearted and possessed of great goodwill."

Again, in January 1906, Tory went west. He presented the British Columbia government with his drafts of two bills, one to found a college, the other to set up its management board. The government introduced them at its next session, January 11. Tory was shocked by the reaction.

Protest meetings were held in Victoria and

**William Osler
The Great Physician**

In 1905 William Osler accepted the post of Regius Professor of Medicine at Oxford: a singular honour, both for Oxford and Osler. For by then he had become one of the all-time giants of medicine – listed with Pasteur and Harvey – and had become known as "the Great Physician." Born in Bond Head, Ont., in 1894, Osler studied in Canada and Europe, and then as a teacher helped make McGill University one of the world's foremost medical schools. His exuberance, personal charm and wisdom attracted support to his efforts to modernize medicine – he brightened up hospital wards, frowned on pill-taking, and taught students to treat the mind as well as the body: psychosomatic medicine. He took students from classroom to patients' bedsides, a method soon copied widely. Through his students and writings he breathed humanity into what was becoming a scientific art. *The Principles of Medicine* (1892), his textbook, sold more than a quarter million copies.

**Helen Gregory McGill
The Judge**

Helen McGill got off to an original start in life, as the first woman graduate in arts from Trinity College, U of T. She grew up in Hamilton, Ont. After graduation in 1890 she spent a busy decade as Japan correspondent for *Cosmopolitan* and *Atlantic Monthly*, reporter and editor. In 1903 she moved to Vancouver and for the next forty years was identified with organizations trying to improve the lot of women and children. In 1917 she was made a judge with Vancouver's Juvenile Court, where she remained until 1945, two years before her death. There McGill backed laws regulating wages and work hours, child labour, old age pension, and raising the age at which men and women could marry. The titles of her two books, *Laws for Women and Children in B.C.* (1912), and *How to Conduct Public Meetings in Canada* (1918), reflect her fundamental interests and concerns.

New Westminster. Ontario's college graduates pressured the premier to dump the bill. "It is too much to say to a Toronto man," said a lawyer, F.C. Wade, "that he cannot have his sons prepared for higher education except on lines dictated by McGill." It was "nothing but an attempt to make BC a feeding ground for McGill," said a Dr. Pearson. "Un-British and vicious," said George Cowan, a prominent lawyer, it "would take our students from our midst and expose them to the vices and prejudices of the effete East."

public-spirited men

The conflict spread to Ontario. President Loudon of Toronto University said the bill was quite unfair since Toronto, "which is a provincial institution, cannot spend money outside the province." Chancellor Burwash of Victoria College called it "a serious injustice . . . to grant McGill University the powers refused to the representatives of the Methodist Church."

Tory made one long and detailed reply in Vancouver's *News Advertiser*. McGill was the only university with the power or desire to help small colleges. Its motive was to raise the level of education in Canada, not, as some people seemed to think, to make money. On every student it taught it lost $300 a year, a loss that had to be met by public-spirited men in Quebec. "I sometimes wonder whether the outlay is justified," Tory said, "when university-trained men can be found who make such statements as have been made during the present discussion."

As the battle reached its climax on February 8 on the floor of the House, the vote revolved around the position of Premier Richard McBride.

"Now, it was alleged," the premier said, "that McGill was to get a preference. Well, if so, she proposed to pay for it. . . . What would be the position if these advantages were repulsed? Toronto

University could not offer them. A provincial university could not give them for many years to come. . . . McGill has done more than all other Canadian institutions put together to give the Dominion a status in the eyes of the educational experts all the world over. What more did the opposition require? Something better? Where would they find it?"

The bill was passed on the third reading. Tory had yet to pick staff and equipment to get the new college open by fall, but his main work was done and he was satisfied.

Back in Montreal he finally decided that he had found his vocation. He resigned from the church and wrote a long letter to Alberta's Premier Rutherford on the danger of letting small church colleges multiply. Then he wangled $50,000 from Andrew Carnegie's new foundation to start building the college in British Columbia. He now had given it a sound financial, legal and administrative base and he could foresee the time – though he didn't know it would take only nine years – when it would become the University of British Columbia.

knew every student's name

In the meantime Premier Rutherford's thoughts on an Alberta university had been stimulated and focussed by Tory's letter. Early in 1907 Rutherford came east looking for a president. In Montreal he inquired about Tory. A rare type, he was told. A thinker who was a leader, a scholar with common sense, a far-sighted man with a firm grasp of detail. He knew every student by name; they came to him constantly for advice. He had won the respect and friendship of his colleagues and such men as W.M. Birks, the jewellery merchant, and John McConnell, the financier-publisher. Over lunch at the Windsor Hotel, the premier asked Tory to come to Edmonton.

Tory was torn. It meant trading Montreal with

its greystone, elm-shaded buildings, where he had expected to spend the rest of his life, for a muddy raw frontier city of 15,000. He asked for time to talk with his wife, who said he should follow his feelings; with Peterson, who said McGill needed him badly; with Dean Charles Moyse, who said that if Tory would stay, he, Moyse, would resign to let Tory become the dean of arts.

They were talking it out when a student, Susan Cameron, passed. Tory turned to her and said more or less jokingly, "What do you say about it? Do I go or stay?"

Seeing a great piece of work being offered to the right man, she cried out excitedly, "But, of course, you must go! It is a tremendous opportunity."

Tory laughed and said, "All right, I am off."

It remained a joke between them. When he saw her in later years he used to say, "You know, *you* sent me out there."

crossfire of rivalry

He arrived in Edmonton in January 1908 to be caught once more in a crossfire of rivalry. Until the influx of gold-seekers bound for the Klondike a decade earlier, Edmonton had been little more than a trading post. Now the jealousy was intense between the new provincial capital and the larger, richer range-land centre of Calgary to the south. Many southern Albertans thought that a university was premature, but if there was going to be one they – most especially R.B. Bennett, a brilliant, brash, belligerent Calgary politician and man of affairs – wanted it in Calgary.

The university was only a word on paper. But in his mind's eye Tory could see it rising from its site, 258 acres of riverside scrubland. He first visited all the high schools to see if students would be forthcoming. To his dismay he found the teachers competitors, each recruiting for his own eastern

Usually a sod-breaking ceremony involves a shiny new shovel. In Alberta, to launch the university's arts building, Premier Rutherford added a western touch by getting behind horses and a plough.

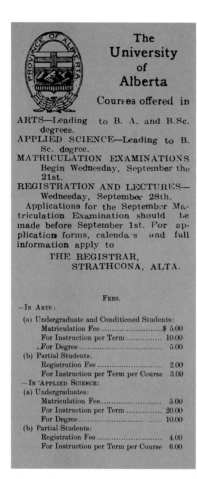
This U of A advertisement appeared in the Medicine Hat Times *in 1910, when the school was just two years old. Its first undergraduates (five women, thirteen men) were still two years away from their degrees.*

Picture day in this grade school finds the class suspiciously well behaved. Right hands on desks, eyes front, no mistakes left on the blackboard. Each pupil's slate with the morning's exercise – draw a sailboat – is displayed along the back wall.

alma mater. But in spite of a Calgary-based campaign to dissuade students from enrolling, Tory lined up thirty to forty potential freshmen.

On a whirlwind trip east he interviewed architects, bought books and equipment, and persuaded four promising young men to come to the frontier. One was Professor E.K. Broadus of Harvard, who later described their lunch in a Boston hotel:

He was telling me of a university that didn't exist, in a province that I had never heard of, in a country that I had never been to, and then and there in an atmosphere of parker-house rolls and staid proprieties, I got an impression which has remained with me ever since as the peculiar essence of Dr. Tory... there was a passion of fulfilment in him. . . . He somehow seemed to belong in a place where things hadn't yet begun and where his restless spirit could loose itself in the doing of them. And he ... made you want to go along and see him do it.

Broadus arrived to find Tory in the attic of a small Strathcona public school. It was a far cry from Harvard. Most of the thirty-seven students who appeared that fall of 1908 were fresh from the farm. They burst into professors' offices and interrupted faculty meetings to ask if their gowns went on over their pants, or where they could buy a pen. They were not prepared for university, and rather than lower standards, the staff spent their evenings in private coaching. Tory also believed in taking the university to the people and he or one of his four professors was constantly on tour. Broadus tells of visiting a small town to find it posted with placards: Come and hear Dr. Broadus lecture on Shakespeare and enjoy yourselves afterwards at the dance.

Next year they moved into an empty floor in a new Strathcona high school. Two of his professors

The University of Alberta's first philosophy class gets set for some mental gymnastics. They all have the appearance of first-rate students: it's hard to imagine any of them day-dreaming or skipping classes. In those days nobody cut classes.

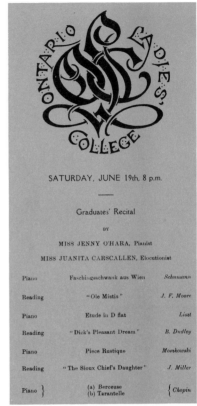

shared an office designed as a lavatory. Tory squeezed a desk and chair into an air shaft. He was now simultaneously upgrading the high school curriculum, designing his buildings and setting up a faculty of agriculture.

On this he was meeting organized opposition. R.B. Bennett and a Calgary dairy farmer named Tregillus were campaigning to have the college of agriculture built in Calgary; then when Tory's project failed the college would become the university. When Tory explained his plans to farm groups, Calgary papers – stirred up by Tregillus – assailed him for "playing politics" by speaking.

The controversy grew so heated that the United Farmers of Alberta asked Tory to talk at their annual meeting in 1910. Tory outlined his dream of a university. It could not be an ivory tower, it had to help solve their problems. To do that it had to be strong. There could not be two

schools fighting for funds, with politicians smearing both, destroying public confidence. The vote was 243 to 7, against separation.

His next fight was to raise professional standards. He rewrote the university act so that anyone starting in professional practice had to pass exams set by university boards. Doctors opposed him bitterly, making a doctor from Texas an issue.Whatever this doctor's training, they argued, Alberta needed doctors.

Tory persuaded Rutherford to investigate the man. His so-called medical school no longer existed and its principal was in jail for selling medical degrees by mail. The story made headlines in 1910, winning the fight for control of standards.

But by fall all Tory's work was facing negation. Premier Rutherford had backed a bushline railway to Fort McMurray and Conservative R.B. Bennett exposed it so scathingly as folly that it killed the project, split the Liberals, and forced Rutherford to resign. Tory had started on his first building on Rutherford's word, without waiting for parliament to vote funds. Now he had to convince the new premier, A.L. Sifton, the brother of Clifford Sifton, that he had spent the $60,000 wisely.

Sifton listened, a cigar clamped in his mouth, staring at Tory for almost an hour, completely, unnervingly silent. When Tory was through all Sifton said was, "You've taken a hell of a lot on yourself."

Tory left, disconcerted and downcast, convinced that Sifton had joined Bennett in planning to shift the university to Calgary. He had not enough money even to pay his staff. But by offering his house as security and getting some businessmen to back him, he managed a bank loan that kept the university open.

Had Bennett now pressed for his agricultural college he would probably have gotten it. Instead,

the Calgary Conservative asked for, and got, a university charter. (The university would begin in the public library in 1912 and fold in three years.) With the Calgarians mollified, with $60,000 already spent, and with Tory's grass-roots support becoming articulate, Sifton found it simpler to back Tory than to block him.

From that turning point in 1910, the University of Alberta grew steadily. Against resistance Tory staffed three schools of agriculture, set up an extension department that grew into the Banff School of Fine Arts, and won a fight for a hospital on the university grounds so that he would one day have a medical faculty. Long ahead of his time Tory foresaw "a world where the requirements of civilization are based essentially on technology."

"The ultimate teaching of all education is just this," he once said, "that every man owes to the generation in which he lives the last full measure of devotion to whatsoever things are true."

Judging by the number of empties on the table, these fraternity revellers have to be on their last legs. Boys will be boys! as mother always said.

Goodbye Dobbin

Robert McLaughlin, the "Governor," was the boss at the McLaughlin Carriage Co.; his strong sense of craftsmanship and responsiblity to customers insured top quality in the company's carriages. His son Sam decided to switch and make cars, and gradually automobiles began sharing space with the horses on the McLaughlin calendars, although the Governor considered them a passing fad. The first autos on the calendars were shown to be unreliable. They were fragile intruders, not up to the hazards of the open road. "Get a horse" and other witticisms were the gibes of the day. But the Governor was wrong: the auto would push Dobbin off the road.

McLaughlin Carriage Co.
OSHAWA, ONT.
Canada's Finest —
"One Grade Only and that the Best."
Our Mikado 35 A

The Only Way to Go

Taking up the new fad–"the infernally combusting engine"–took courage. Patience and a spirit of adventure were as important as a well-stocked tool box. Early tires, for example, were flimsy affairs, and punctures (nobody called them flats then) were common. You had to know how to use the things in your trunk: patch kits, wrenches and the good old crank. Those who ventured too far often found themselves miles from the nearest garage. By the end of the decade, rules of the road and speed limits were being enforced in most cities and towns, usually by police on bicycles or horses. In Ontario the limit was "7 m.p.h. within 100 yards of a horse," with a penalty of $25 or 30 days in jail for reckless violators.

On hot dusty motoring outings this Eaton's fan came in handy.

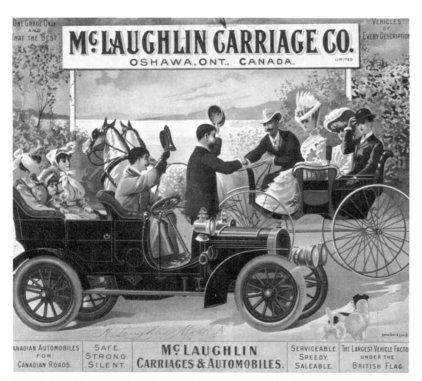

The McLaughlin model A on this calendar never got off the designer's drawing board.

"Guess they didn't know 'twas a McLaughlin," quips the nonchalant carriage driver.

66

While sensible car makers were improving gas-driven cars, two American brothers were selling "Stanley Steamers." This troupe is heading for Kentville N.S. in one.

Snobs of the horse and carriage set watch with a touch of pity (and a dash of superiority) as the unreliable jalopy proves its worthlessness once again.

CHAPTER SIX

Col. Sam and the Horseless Carriage

The McLaughlins used to joke that "Sam has wheels in his head."

Sam McLaughlin

Glumly they watched as flames dissolved the factory that was their livelihood – Sam McLaughlin, his brother George, their father Robert ("the Governor"), and six hundred Oshawa employees.

By month's end, the last month of the century, they were jubilantly comparing offers of loans to rebuild from fifteen Ontario communities: a striking affirmation of faith in a firm and an industry.

The McLaughlin Carriage Company, founded thirty-three years before by Robert McLaughlin, was rebuilt in Oshawa with the latest innovations: an electric generator, a telephone and a water-pump. It also had the first female secretary in town. In 1900 the company sold 25,000 carriages. It had branches in the Maritimes and the far Saskatchewan frontier. It was selling in distant Australia and South America. Junior partner Sam McLaughlin was one of Canada's busiest young men; the designer for a company that offered 143 models, from democrats for farmers to fancy phaetons for city folk. Thirty years old, Sam McLaughlin had never seen a car.

He knew about them, of course. You could not read a newspaper and not know about the car, pioneered in Europe in the eighties, and now hammered together in fifty-odd shops throughout North America by plumber's supply men like David Buick, wagon builders like Clem Studebaker, axle makers like Harry Stutz. Almost weekly the sports pages headlined a new speed record set by Barney Oldfield, or Alexander Winton, or Henry Ford. Two Toronto ladies had made news just by driving a gas-powered car down Yonge Street.

Cars were the latest toys of the rich, the sporting set. William K. Vanderbilt had a car that had cost him $18,000. King Edward drove with an engineer who sat beside the chauffeur. His beautiful Queen Alexandra had her own electric "Victorlette" which would travel forty miles on one battery charge. There was even a magazine called *The Horseless Age.*

But the automobile – some preferred the elegant French word – was simply froth on the surface of a horse-and-carriage world. The characteristic sound of the times was the clip-clop of horses' hoofs, the most stirring sight a fire engine careening behind four galloping chargers. The car merely copied the carriage; some cars even had imitation whip-sockets. Most people thought cars were objectionably noisy and unreliable. When they backfired, horses bolted and ladies fell off their bicycles. A favourite school debate was "Resolved: That the Motor-car is Useless, Dangerous, and Ought to be Abolished." When U. K. Dandurand applied to

Helmet, goggles, speed, a pretty lady watching on – what better reasons could there be for buying a new roadster?

**Sam McLaughlin
"The Colonel"**

In 1907, when the first McLaughlin car rolled out of an Oshawa carriage shop, Sam McLaughlin must have been proud – and a little nervous. He had backed the notion that cars were here to stay, something his father, the "Governor," founder of the family business, thought was poppycock. But Sam was right, and before long his luxurious custom-made autos were puttering along rough Canadian streets. Everything but the engines were Canadian-made, for these Sam went to Will Durant in Detroit. By the end of WW I he had wheeled and dealed himself into a fortune, but the days of the McLaughlin were numbered. As demand increased, smaller innovative manufacturers gradually sold their designs and patents to the larger firms, and in 1918 the McLaughlin line became part of General Motors. In his 100-year lifetime the "Colonel" made his quarter-billion nevertheless.

Well after automobiles had invaded the right of way, draught horses, like these in Arnprior, were keeping milliners in business.

the city of Montreal for a car licence the clerk issued him two bicycle permits. Why set up a new procedure for a passing fad?

It might have been 1902 or 1903 – recalling it later, McLaughlin could not be sure – when company bookkeeper Oliver Hezzlewood proudly drove to work in a car. It was built of "air-seasoned timber" bolted to buggy wheels and it steered from the right, because in a buggy you drove from the right. To start it, Hezzlewood adjusted the spark and gas levers then heaved on the crank with his ear cocked for the first sputter of the motor. When it caught he dashed back – if he was still on his feet – pushed the levers to "idling" – a high-decibel state of violent shuddering – kicked out the clutch and jerked away. Like all cars, except limousines, it was open, which made it, Hezzlewood said, "a little inconvenient in inclement weather."

He meant that when it rained he got soaked. So McLaughlin made him a rubberized sheet that fitted over the body, with four holes through which the passengers stuck their heads. Hezzlewood was so pleased that he let Sam drive the car. "From then on I had a new kind of wheels in my head," McLaughlin said, "motor-driven wheels."

McLaughlin convinced his brother George that the car had a future. But he could not convince the Governor. Robert McLaughlin agreed with the editor who saw the car as a "locomotive running wildly in the streets," something that "would never be permitted to supplant the ordinary forms of conveyance."

At the St. Louis World's Fair in 1904, one hundred cars were shown: one hundred mechanically-minded men all scrambling for backers. By 1905 it was clear to Sam McLaughlin that time was running out. David Buick's company, financed by

These horses are struggling through the mud of Toronto's St. Clair Avenue, pulling a small, ornate child's hearse.

T. A. Russell
Aristocrat of the Road

Canadian carriage maker William Patterson, was two years old. So was Henry Leland's Cadillac company and Henry Ford's company, backed by Detroit coal dealer Alex Malcolmson. Some Windsor men had started a Ford assembly plant the year before. The Packard company had just opened in St. Catharines. And Ransom Eli Olds was making his car "for the masses," a little one-cylinder two-seater selling at $650, "including mudguards." In the last four years Olds had sold 12,000 cars, inspiring the new Gus Edwards' song "In My Merry Oldsmobile." Sam decided to spend his 1905 vacation exploring the field.

Without telling his father, he toured the Thomas Flyer plant in Detroit, the Peerless plant in Cleveland and the Pierce-Arrow plant in Buffalo. Mr. Pierce, forecasting his own demise in the thirties, startled him by saying, "Cars like this have no future." They were too big, too expensive at

$3,000. Like most car makers except Olds, Mr. Pierce sold from one sample then handcrafted his cars as orders came in.

The Thomas Flyer, McLaughlin found, was already under franchise to the Canada Cycle and Motor Company in Toronto. He hurried to Jackson, Michigan, home of axle maker Charles Lewis, whose Jackson had just won the hundred-mile Vanderbilt Cup race on Long Island. During breakfast at the Jackson hotel, William Durant walked in. "Sam!" Durant exclaimed, "What on earth are you doing here?"

Durant was an important American carriage maker who had just bought the Buick company; McLaughlin had met him often at conventions. As McLaughlin explained, Durant listened, then said, "Charlie Lewis is a dear friend of mine. You get his story. Then if you're not satisfied, come and see me."

Lewis was a fine old gentleman, friendly and

"Tommy" Russell was the standout Canadian patriot in the world of early "auto-motion," as general manager of CCM, and later with the Russell Motor Company (owned by CCM). An early car was sold with the ad "The Thoroughly Canadian Car"– it used Canadian material, labour, and capital. CCM noticed Russell's executive ability soon after his graduation from the University of Toronto in 1899, hired him, and soon made him general manager. His shrewdness showed in his decision to buy the much-maligned Knight engine in 1909, giving him an ultra-modern power source to go with the Russell's luxurious features. By 1910 the Russell had become the last word in luxury on Canadian roads. But the 1913 Russell-Knight proved unreliable, sales fell off, and the Russell name was tarnished. In 1915 Willys-Overland, an American firm, bought Russell – a bitter ending for Canada's first really successful automobile.

Touring

With the motor car, a new word–"touring"–came into the vocabulary of Canadians. On Saturday and Sunday afternoons, mom would pack the kids into the back seat, dad would give the starting crank a turn, and off they would go for a drive in the country. As the cloud of dust came nearer, farmers would lean on their hay rakes, scratch their heads and wonder what the city folks would think of next. But in time they would find themselves at the wheel, heading for a tour of the city.

H.N. Eaton's gas station on Doyle Street, Halifax, was the first in Nova Scotia. Out front are some McKay cars, made in the province. Their steering wheels had a habit of coming off in the driver's hands.

The giant cedars of Vancouver's Stanley Park dwarf the autos in this 1904 car rally. These pioneer motorists still bought gas by the bucket from hardware stores.

72

Bill Dobie of Pincher Creek, Alta., thought there would be a fierce demand for the five-wheeled Glover in Alberta, but that extra wheel just buried his investment.

This motorized street cleaner was just one of the many specialized vehicles made in the decade. By 1907 there were motor buses, mail trucks, and the first snowmobile was only a few years away.

informative, eager to have a new outlet for his Jackson. McLaughlin ordered two for testing by Hezzlewood and himself.

Driving was an adventure in 1905; a twenty-mile drive was a conversation piece. Outside cities the roads were improved dirt or unimproved dirt. In summer the dust was so blinding that passengers wore goggles and dusters. In spring the mud was axle-deep and some farmers made a living hauling motorists out of potholes (which the farmers themselves kept watered). On cloudy days a man drove with one eye on the ruts and the other skyward; it took fifteen minutes to get up the canvas top and the side curtains. And after a rain the car slithered and skidded and ended up mired in mud, the engine coughing, gasping and belching steam. Every driver carried a towrope, blowout patches and a full tool kit. The song "Get Out and Get Under" was a hit because it hit home.

broke down too often

But even by 1905 standards, the Jacksons broke down too often. "If we had not been optimists," McLaughlin later recalled, "we would have gone contentedly back to carriage making." Instead he took the train to Toronto and paid $1,650 for a two-cylinder Model F Buick. Before he had driven to Oshawa he knew he had found his car. He wired Durant and reminded him of his offer. In Durant's New York office they haggled for hours without reaching agreement. There was not much money involved but neither would give in.

Back in Oshawa Sam told his father of his venture and its failure, expecting him to say, "All right, that's over, let's get busy making carriages." Instead he listened while George and Sam worked out an alternative plan – they would make their own car. All the Governor said was, "If you think you can make a go of it, go ahead." The carriage business was big enough to give his boys a flyer.

Their first vital need was a first-rate engineer. They finally settled on Arthur Milbrath from Milwaukee. He supervised the installing of lathes, machine tools, planers, shapers, and had parts custom-built in Cleveland for a car with more power than the Buick. McLaughlin worked nights throughout 1906 on the body design and the radiator emblem. Then in September of 1907, with the parts for a hundred cars on the factory floor and parts for another hundred nearing completion, Milbrath was confined to bed with pleurisy.

the project died

Without Milbrath the project was dead. McLaughlin wired Durant, asking to borrow an engineer. Instead, Durant appeared the next day with two executives but no engineer. Picking up the discussion of two years before as if he had just paused for breath, Durant outlined a fifteen-year deal that allowed the McLaughlins to buy Buick engines.

"That will work," McLaughlin said.

"I thought it would," Durant replied.

No mention was made of the two hundred cars lying unborn on the plant floor. The lathes could perhaps be sold but everything else would have to be scrapped. In the elder McLaughlin's office it took them five minutes to sign the contract that would transform McLaughlin's career, company and hometown.

He had got in just in time – the transitional year of the infant industry. Henry Leland put interchangeable parts in his Cadillacs that year, introducing precision tooling for machine parts. And that October the stock market fell and the sale of big cars slumped, while sales of Ford's low-priced Model S quintupled.

These events decided Henry Ford to stake everything he had on an idea so dismaying that his general manager quit. To the joy of his competi-

Motor Fashion

Driving in the warm months invited a dust bath. The stuff settled over car and occupants and worked its way into pockets, eyes, everywhere. So motorists fought back with goggles, huge hats, and long "dusters" worn over clothing.

*Toronto's Thomas Roulston still had
a few good business years ahead, but
many of his potential clients were
already going a few doors down the
street for some* real *driving lessons.*

*Opposite page: Market day in Montreal's
Jacques Cartier Square. Cars, trucks
and horse-drawn wagons deliver and
take home bottles, boxes, bags and
baskets filled with all manner of
merchandise. Horses were used in this
sort of work for several more decades.*

tors he announced that from now on he would
produce only a single model: a simple, rugged,
light, cheap car for "the great multitude," as he
put it, to enjoy "God's great open spaces." Each
car would be alike "as one pin is like another pin"
and any customer could have "a car painted any
colour that he wants so long as it is black."

In 1909 the first Model Ts came rolling off an
"assembly line." They had standard parts, as did
the Oldsmobile and Cadillac. Ford priced his car
at $950, and he was able to cut the price every year
as production rose.

To his rivals' chagrin, the Model T outsold all
other makes combined. It was the farmer's car, the
average man's car, the beloved Tin Lizzie, the pud-
dle jumper, the famous flivver. Catalogues listing
its interchangeable parts built a mail-order business; it wrote *finis* to the life of companies who
could not see its significance.

the Ivanhoe went under

In 1909 there were 743 plants in North America making cars; two years later only 270 were left,
and for a Canadian, an American tie-in was no
guarantee of success. In those early days of the car
more than a thousand makes came and went,
including the Moose Jaw Standard of Saskatchewan, the LeRoy of Kitchener, the Russell-Knight
of Toronto, the Crow, the Ivanhoe, the Briscoe.
From 1909 on, none would survive that could not
be mass-produced. By judgement and luck, Sam
McLaughlin had picked a winner.

In 1909 his friend Will Durant merged Buick,
Olds (and later Cadillac) in a New Jersey holding
company called General Motors. (Durant could
and would have bought Ford that year for $9.5
million in cash if his bankers hadn't said it wasn't
worth it.) Sam McLaughlin remained a vice-presi-
dent of the parent American company as Durant
lost control and recaptured it, only to lose it again

to the DuPonts.

As General Motors grew, so did the McLaughlins. Their McLaughlin-Buick was so distinctively
designed that a visiting General Motors executive
once ordered one shipped to the New York head
office. It was parked in front of the showroom
when President Alfred Sloan came in. "Get that
thing out of here," he said, "and quick! It's gather-
ing crowds – and it's no more like one of our
Buicks than a St. Bernard is like a dachshund!"

first gas station

By 1910 Sam McLaughlin could foresee the
end of the Governor's business. Motorists still
bought gas by the bucketful in stores or livery sta-
bles but Imperial Oil had opened the first service
station in Vancouver in 1908. Courtship still took
place under Mama's eyes in the parlour and food
was "put up" in the cellar every fall, but the instrument that would change all this was pushing the
horse off the road. Few young men were training
as blacksmiths or harness makers; they were learning new trades in rubber, glass, magnetos, batter-
ies, concrete, asphalt, alloys, machining, trucking
and advertising.

Thanks to Oliver Hezzlewood's hankering after
a horseless carriage, however, and the incident of
an engineer falling ill, the McLaughlin Carriage
Company would become, five years later, the General Motors Company of Canada.

In his lifetime as company president, then
chairman, Sam McLaughlin would see long rib-
bons of concrete unrolling across the nation, re-
casting the work patterns, attitudes and morals of
the continent, altering the family structure, the
landscape, the atmosphere. And in his nineties,
still "in harness" – a phrase retained in the horseless age – he would daily pass by the factory he
had helped rebuild in 1900, a reminder of the way
it had all begun.

That's Entertainment

Live theatre used to thrill thousands of Canadians from coast to coast before movies took over. A theatrical touring system called "the Road" brought top-ranked troupes to theatres across the country.

In this children's pageant in Victoria, B.C., the good fairies are dressed in stars, the goblins are clearly bad, and the music – only the audience can tell if it's good or bad.

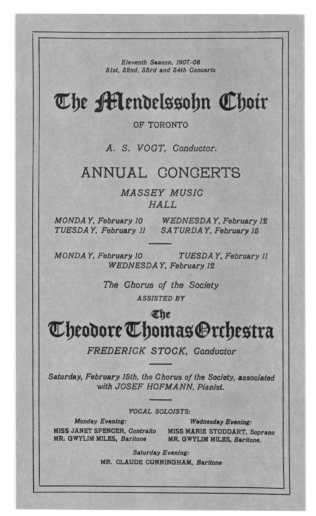

Eleventh Season, 1907-08
31st, 32nd, 33rd and 34th Concerts

The Mendelssohn Choir
OF TORONTO

A. S. VOGT, Conductor.

ANNUAL CONCERTS

MASSEY MUSIC HALL

MONDAY, February 10   WEDNESDAY, February 12
TUESDAY, February 11   SATURDAY, February 15

MONDAY, February 10   TUESDAY, February 11
WEDNESDAY, February 12

The Chorus of the Society

ASSISTED BY

The Theodore Thomas Orchestra

FREDERICK STOCK, Conductor

Saturday, February 15th, the Chorus of the Society, associated with JOSEF HOFMANN, Pianist.

VOCAL SOLOISTS:

Monday Evening: Wednesday Evening:
MISS JANET SPENCER, Contralto   MISS MARIE STODDART, Soprano
MR. GWYLIM MILES, Baritone   MR. GWYLIM MILES, Baritone.

Saturday Evening:
MR. CLAUDE CUNNINGHAM, Baritone

The Toronto Mendelssohn Choir advertises its eleventh season. Founder A.S. Vogt conducted the choir until 1917.

Moving pictures first came to Cardston, Alta., with the Palace cinema, seen here in 1907. Cinemas spread quickly. Montreal's and Toronto's first theatres had opened just the previous year.

"Who do you have to know to get served in this joint?" could well be the outburst from the excited actor on the right, in this drawing room comedy at the Winnipeg Theatre.

Stiff-as-starch soldiers sport well-starched, huge fake moustaches. Other actors in this French-Canadian stage production wear outfits of 18th century dandies, priests, and adventurers.

TEMPLE OF FAME
OPERA HOUSE
Friday Evening, April 20th, 1900
Programme

GODDESS..........................MISS ARCHER
  Attendants. Mrs. A. Stevenson, Miss Lundy
CANADA...........................Miss Sherwood
WILHELMINA, QUEEN OF HOLLAND..Miss Pearl Lundy
POCAHONTAS........................Miss L Rush
JENNIE LIND...................Miss F. Belleghem
BICYCLE GIRL............ ....Miss Madge Davidson
FLORENCE NIGHTENGALE...........Miss M. Donnel
JAPAN... ....Miss G. Kendry
QUEEN OF SHEBA.....................Miss Belcher
SISTER OF CHARITY..........Miss M. Sawers
CLEOPATRA.......................Miss Rackham
TABITHA PRIMROSE.........Miss A. Burnham
MAGGIE MUCKLEPACKET...........Miss Carnegie
SAPPHO.....................Miss S. Stethem
GRACE DARLING.......... ....Miss D. Comstock
JOAN OF ARC........... ......Miss L. Moore
ELIZABETH, QUEEN OF ENGLAND.. ....Miss Halliday
FLORA McDONALD...................Miss N. Hall
HELEN OF TROY.......... ....Miss N. Davies
MRS. PARTINGTON and IKE..Miss Gertrude Clarry and
                              Raymond Homan
RUTH..........................   ....Mrs. Seward
TOPSY....   ....R. Stone
MOTHER GOOSE & LITTLE MISS MUFFET........
    ....Misses D. Bell & N. Graham
TWENTIETH CENTURY GIRL ....Mrs Bradburn
MOTHER AND CHILDREN........Mrs. A. H. Stratton
                    Wilfred Stratton and Dorothy Hill
QUEEN VICTORIA..... .... Mrs J. H. McClellan
  PAGES.... ...... Holden & Walter Blackwell
  GUARDS......Messrs. Hammond, Houston,
              Gladman, Brundrett, Sawers,
              Lundy.
  HERALDS......Messrs. Milburn and Cluxton.
  ACCOMPANISTS....Messrs. Crane and Walden.
  CROWN BEARER................Helen Rush

The cast of roles for the Peterborough, Ontario, program reads like the roll call of history's second coming.

CHAPTER SEVEN

The Million-Dollar Northern Stakes

"For we'll sing a little song of Cobalt,
If you don't live there it's your fault."

The Cobalt Song

They were cutting through rock at sunset a hundred miles north of North Bay, laying their rails on the primal stone of the Shield. It had been rock, rock all the way, the hardest rock in the world, a colossal mountain range ground into hummocks by two billion years of erosion, its rises bristling with tangled pine, its hollows brimming with water, sometimes choked with the half-living, sponge-like vegetation known as muskeg.

In his blacksmith's shack by the shining new rails, Alfred LaRose was sharpening drill bits. He looked out at the sun-flushed rockcut. Its veins had a strange pink tint. (Legend has it he had bared it the night before when he threw his hammer at what he thought were the eyes of a fox.) He strolled over and knocked off three chunks of rock.

He showed them next day to Duncan McMartin, the government contractor. Ten surveys three years before, in 1900, had reported potential farmland beneath the bush at the north end of Lake Timiskaming, and the province was building this railway, the Timiskaming and Northern Ontario, from North Bay to the lakeside towns of Haileybury and New Liskeard, where a few dozen families struggled for a living on their clearings and a few frame buildings fronted a wooden sidewalk.

McMartin looked at the pinkish bloom of the rocks. He knew only what everyone else knew of the Shield: that it was worthless except for furs and whatever timber hadn't been logged off by the Booth and Gillies companies down at Ottawa. The railway would never pay for a mile of its 110 miles of rockwork. It had been an election promise, rashly made and now hopefully justified as a "colonization road" that would bring in settlers. This was Indian and blackfly country. Prospectors had by-passed it; it hadn't even been mapped by geologists. Gold was "geologically impossible," and silver was found only in the tropics. McMartin handed the rocks back. "Very nice, Alfred," he said, noncommittally.

LaRose kept talking it up all through September. Some of the road gang thought it could be copper. McMartin kept thinking about it. The geologists could be wrong. On the CPR line just west of here they had found copper and nickel, the biggest nickel lode in the world, and this was the same kind of granite. McMartin finally advised LaRose to stake a claim, paid $1,500 for a half-interest, and sent samples to the Ontario Bureau of Mines.

With cash in his pocket, LaRose decided to visit his hometown of Hull. On his way he stopped at Mattawa, a CPR branch-line junction on the old fur-trade trail up the Ottawa River. Its single dusty street was lined with two-storey wooden buildings:

The front cover of the Canadian Courier *shows the humble beginnings of the multi-million dollar mining business that boomed around Cobalt.*

Opposite page: One of the biggest mining stampedes in history brought thousands of city-slicker greenhorns, veteran prospectors and others to the silver camp of Cobalt – a jumble of shacks, mines and twisting roads.

While miners were cashing in on the Canadian Shield's silver and gold, real estate brokers were cashing in on the miners. In ten years the population jumped to 30,000: a realtor's gold mine.

houses, bootleg and gambling joints, brothels, a hotel. LaRose was full of his find and the hotel-man, Arthur Firland, sent him to see his broth-er-in-law, Noah Timmins.

Noah and his brother Henry, who was then visiting Ottawa, ran northeastern Ontario's biggest store, the last frontier supply-post east of North Bay. Like their father before them, the Timmins brothers were known throughout the area as men who would gamble a grubstake on any show of colour. LaRose tossed his samples on the counter.

believed in the Shield

Noah Timmins was one of the few who be-lieved in the Shield. He had heard Indians talk of silver, and silver worth $3.5 million had been found in 1868 on Skull Rock in Lake Superior. He studied the samples. They seemed impregnated with metal that could be silver. He shrugged and pushed the ore back across the counter.

LaRose left, a little crestfallen. Noah tele-graphed Henry in Ottawa, and Henry intercepted LaRose. As Noah had reckoned, LaRose was more inclined now to make a deal. For $3,500 the Timmins brothers bought half of LaRose's half-in-terest, only to find that a man named King, backed by a millionaire Renfrew contractor, M. J. O'Brien, had restaked their claim.

It was a portent of all the excitement to come, the activity that would change forever the nature of the Shield. LaRose's rocks had duly arrived at the Bureau of Mines in Toronto and Willet Miller, the provincial geologist, had taken one look and set off up the Ottawa. He found the rockcut staked by LaRose at the north end of Long Lake. Its veins revealed silver interlaced with a rare metal called cobalt. At the south end of the lake he met James McKinley and Ernest Darragh. They had been hunting timber for railroad ties earlier that summer and had noted streaks of white metal in the cliff face. They could gouge it out with their penknives, dent it with their teeth.

"Silver!" Miller told them. "Native silver." In the rubble at the cliff base he found to his astonishment pieces of black tarnished silver "as large," he said later, "as stove lids or cannonballs." Back at the site of LaRose's find, he scratched "This is Cobalt" on a board and anchored it in a rock cairn. There was no doubt in Miller's mind that this would be big.

By November, half the road gang were drilling and blasting the rocks for ore. The LaRose strike was restaked by King, and a man named Tom Hebert found a rich vein. The Timmins group had cut in Dave Dunlap, a Mattawa lawyer, to handle their lawsuit, which he won. But when Noah tried to borrow $5,000 to start digging ore, the bank in Haileybury turned him down. The Shield was "wasteland." Only two years before, the London *Times* had declared that Canadians were silly "to dig holes in the ground in hopes that Canada may at some time produce a few odd ounces of precious metals."

filled with nuggets

The following spring a businessman named George Trethewey came in from Edmonton and at dusk staked what became the Coniagas. He set up the first machinery: a boiler and a hoist. But when he went to Toronto, his pockets filled with nuggets, and told his mining friends of the wealth of the Shield, they looked at him, he later recalled, with "a sort of pity."

Unable to find backing they began to mine it themselves – Trethewey, Hebert, McKinley and Darragh, and the LaRose-Timmins group – gouging the ore from the surface veins with dynamite, hand-drill and pick. In a month the Timmins group had forty tons. They bagged it, loaded two freight cars and shipped it to Jersey City where

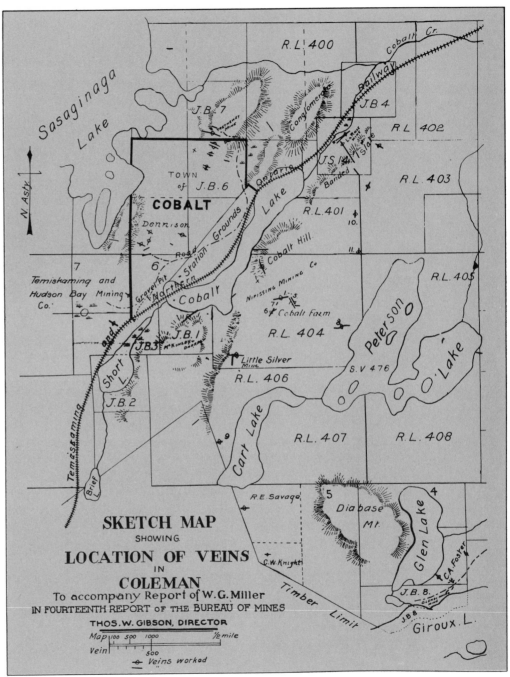

The T & NO Railway ("Time No Object," some called it) pushed into the forbidding Shield in 1902. Later its trains, loaded with minerals and pulp, were called "Hundred Million Dollar Specials."

This branch line poked into the Porcupine region late in the decade. Some fortune-seekers had the misfortune to ride north in hastily-built passenger cars bolstered with rough-hewn logs and siding. As in most gold rushes, the majority struck it poor.

When Noah (top) and Henry (bottom) Timmins bought the La Rose mine they turned their backs on storekeeping in Mattawa, Ont., for good. They developed the Hollinger mine into a fabulous fortune, and left their name on the nearby town of Timmins.

Noah sold it to the Leduc Chemical and Reduction Works. On his return he waved the cheque beneath the Haileybury banker's nose. It was for $40,000, and the bank had lost the account.

Apathy vanished. The *New York World* reported a strike "which promises to prove one of the richest in the world." In 1904 ore worth $200,000 was shipped from Cobalt's mines. The next spring the Guggenheims and the Rockefellers bought in. Timmins invested his earnings in an option on five nearby claims. A month later he sold them for $600,000. The rush was on.

Overnight the ambling one-coach railroad became the "Cobalt Flyer" with fourteen cars. Every day it disgorged a fevered crowd of promoters, speculators, lawyers, miners, surveyors, geologists, engineers. Sourdoughs who had risked death to reach the Klondike gold camp a few years before came to Cobalt by Pullman car. The station was piled with their packs and canoes, the hillside was tiered with their camps. They crowded the Bank of Commerce tent, where a packing case served as a counter, queued up for the prostitutes' tents, kept the gamblers' tents glowing nightly. But here, as in the Klondike, the Mounted Police and the Mining Court made gunslinging and sandbagging unprofitable.

By 1906 the area was staked out in thousands of claims. Five hundred and eighty-four companies had been formed. A town of seven thousand had sprung up, crisscrossed with trenches and wooden steps running up and down the hills and around the headframes of the mines. An acre of marshland that had sold two years before for 10 cents was now selling for thousands of dollars. Any vein with a stain of cobalt could be sold for thousands of dollars. One farmer came into town, recalled seeing that cobalt bloom, and walked

At first only veins of the richest ores were mined, and valuable tailings were dumped into Cobalt Lake or piled up around the countryside. These heaps grow outside the Hudson Bay Mine in Cobalt. Tailings were later re-worked for their ore.

Spectacular Samples of Porcupine Gold

Exhibitions of Specimens from the Wilson Claims in the New Gold District

To be Sent to Toronto.

Mr. W. S. Edwards, of Chicago, who holds the controlling interest in the Wilson claims at Porcupine is a guest at the Matabanick Hotel in Haileybury and the exhibition of samples from the new gold fields which he has with him is causing considerable excitement around the camp.

He came up from Toronto last week and met Jack Wilson his partner coming down from Porcupine with a large number of samples from his main vein. These are to be placed on exhibition in the King Edward hotel in Toronto within a short time. The gold is shown in all the various kinds of quartz and schist found in that country and some of the samples are worth several hundred dollars each just for the amount of gold they contain and not as specimens.

The Cobalt News-Herald *plays up some new samples from Porcupine, one of the great spin-off strikes from Cobalt.*

back fifteen miles to stake the Casey Cobalt; it yielded $2.5 million in silver.

Silver flowed out onto the surface and a passerby was killed by a prospector blasting a testhole on Cobalt's main street. The Lawson Mine had a surface vein that was polished like a mirror by people walking on it to feel a million dollars. Using hand picks, miners extracted nuggets that looked like dinner plates, sea shells and bath sponges; one nugget measured three by six feet and was worth $6,000. In the underground stopes writhing under the streets there was flake silver, leaf silver, hair silver. The twelve square miles around Cobalt were the world's richest silver camp, producing more silver than all the mines in Montana put together, rivalling the fabled mines of Peru and Mexico.

Shares in the Timiskaming and Hudson's Bay Company soared from 40 cents in 1905 to 40 dollars in 1906. Demand for Cobalt stock grew so strong that on a few days that summer the police were called out to handle the crowds on Wall Street. Brokerage companies began in Toronto on the strength of a claim or two picked up on a quick trip to Cobalt. Toronto brokers had never known such electrifying activity. The King Edward Hotel bar was the financial centre of the north. "From a people that nothing could move," Trethewey told a reporter, "we now have a mad clamouring crowd buying everything in the form of Cobalt stock – the end of which spells disaster for many."

More than 500 companies eventually failed after raising tens of millions of dollars. But Cobalt by 1909 was big business. In some thirty mines a thousand drills fed by giant air compressors were annually digging out silver worth $20 million, plus 2,000 tons of cobalt, used for ceramics. Cobalt had 30,000 people, and was linked by electric tram to

**Benny Hollinger
The Barber Who Struck It Rich**

Benny Hollinger was a teenage barber in Haileybury, Ont., when the Cobalt silver scramble began. With a pal, Alex Gillis, he decided to try his luck on the Canadian Shield and set about raising a grubstake. Gillis raised $100. Hollinger found $150, which he got from Jack McMahon, a bartender willing to take a risk. The pair set out from Haileybury and late in 1909 stumbled across a pit that changed their lives: the dirt there was shot through with gold. They left the assayers' office aglow, rushed back and staked six claims. Noah Timmins heard of the strike and sight unseen bought Hollinger's claims for $330,000, a high price for the times. Hollinger took his money and disappeared, but his name did not: the Hollinger mine became the second biggest gold producer in Canada.

Haileybury, where forty silver kings lived on a lakeshore road known as "Millionaire's Row." The Cobalt brokerage office was "the little Bay Street of the Northland." On every corner were hotels, their corridors lined with cots, for almost every businessman, professional man and bootlegger was grubstaking one or more prospectors. Cobalt had become the base for a great assault on the Shield.

thousands of men

More than a thousand prospectors fanned out from Cobalt, travelling by steam launch, motorboat, sailboat, canoe – an army of men sizing up formations, digging, drilling, staking. Their finds flashed across the headlines: Elk Lake, Gowganda, Larder Lake. But no big mines resulted until later. As Cobalt's *Northern Miner* put it then: "The money put into this region has passed mainly into the pockets of the promoters and of the newspapers who will play up any company advertising in their pages."

Among the prospectors was Benny Hollinger, the nineteen-year-old nephew of an ex-bartender and locomotive engineer, Jack McMahon. Jack had struck it rich in silver and that summer of 1909 he "chucked away $150," he told his brothers-in-law, "on a grubstake for young Benny and might as well have thrown it out the window." His brothers-in-law – Jack, Charlie and Gilbert La-Bine – chipped in $75 for a half-interest in Benny.

By September Benny Hollinger and his partner Alex Gillis had reached Porcupine Lake, deep in the wilderness. They were the third group to reach the lake that season. Tom Geddes and George Bannerman had come in and found gold in August. Paddling out to record their claims they had passed a party of four paddling in. The four men had camped that night on a dome-shaped hill. In the morning Harry Preston had slipped and skid-

ded down the hill. He had stopped cursing when he saw that his heels had stripped the moss off a quartz vein. Now Preston and his partners told Benny and Alex to move on.

Farther up the lake, on October 4, Gillis was cutting a claim stake and Benny was pulling the moss off the rocks when, as Gillis later described it:

. . . suddenly he let a roar out of him and threw his hat to me. At first I thought he was crazy but when I came over to where he was at, the quartz where he had taken off the moss looked as though someone had dipped a candle along it, but instead of wax it was gold.

They staked three claims, tossed for choice, and Benny won. Back in Haileybury Jack McMahon was incoherent with excitement. A howling mob was launching a gold rush sparked by Geddes and Bannerman. McMahon told Noah Timmins, who cornered him in a hotel, that he wouldn't sell out for less than $1 million.

gold rush launched

Noah let him cool off while he hustled his engineer-nephew, Alphonse Paré, up to Porcupine to look over Benny's claim. Paré told him to buy, but Noah's partners, Duncan McMartin and Henry Timmins, balked. Gold in Ontario? It sounded like a pipedream. But as Noah decided to go it alone Henry said quietly, "I'm with you." For $330,000 they bought what became the Hollinger; and an American group bought Preston's find, which became the Dome.

Timmins at times must have regretted it. Porcupine was a high-cost camp. The motherlode was buried deep and the heavy drilling equipment had to be sledded in across lake ice that broke under its weight thirteen times. It was two difficult years before the skips would bring up gold.

There are only two bottles between these 19 prospectors; clearly they hadn't struck it rich yet. Many of the men who trooped north knew nothing about prospecting, and even the veterans generally were not experts in geology. Their edge over the beginners was more in their ability to travel and live in the wilderness.

Workers in the melting house in Ottawa's new Royal Mint pour molten gold into molds for ingots.

But the Hollinger mined, in its first year, almost $1 million in gold and the Dome, at peak production, shipped $1 million in bullion a month. "The Golden Stairway," they called the Dome, and when it was finally dug out they called its hilltop crater "The Glory Hole." These two mines, plus another mine peddled for peanuts by prospector Sandy McIntyre, produced gold worth nearly $1 billion and proved that Cobalt was not an isolated find.

spread like veins

The Cobalt fortunes spread through Canadian mining like veins in high-grade. Charles Dennison, a backer of Cobalt's Nipissing Silver Mine, put his money into development of the famous Tech-Hughes Gold Mine. Gilbert LaBine collected $27,500 for his $25 share in Benny Hollinger, and with it found gold in Manitoba and pitchblende on Great Bear Lake. Noah Timmins moved to Montreal but his money remained in the North. It developed the San Antonio Mine in Manitoba, Chromium Mining and Smelting in Sault Ste. Marie. It would later save Noranda Mines from bankruptcy and open the gigantic iron reserves of Labrador.

Cobalt triggered a chain reaction. The needs of its mines for power put hydroelectric plants on the Montreal, Englehart and Matabichouan rivers. The experience gained at Cobalt by prospectors, engineers and mining men cracked open the Shield from Val d'Or to Flin Flon. Within ten years of LaRose's strike, Toronto was shipping north supplies worth $75 million a year. By then the burgeoning towns of the Shield had opened its clay belt for farming and Cobalt had paid for its railway five times over. Cobalt transformed mining from a series of happy incidents into an expanding stable industry and gave Toronto the world's biggest mining market.

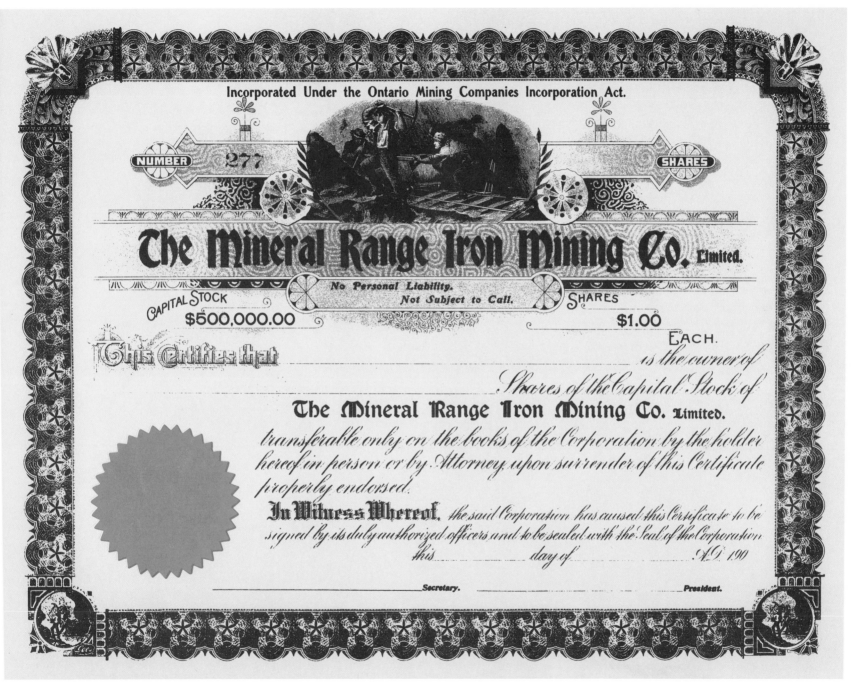

Incorporated Under the Ontario Mining Companies Incorporation Act.

NUMBER 277 SHARES

The Mineral Range Iron Mining Co. Limited.

No Personal Liability.
Not Subject to Call.

CAPITAL STOCK
$500,000.00

SHARES
$1.00 EACH.

This Certifies that _____ is the owner of

_____ Shares of the Capital Stock of

The Mineral Range Iron Mining Co. Limited.

transferable only on the books of the Corporation by the holder hereof in person or by Attorney, upon surrender of this Certificate properly endorsed.

In Witness Whereof, the said Corporation has caused this Certificate to be signed by its duly authorized officers and to be sealed with the Seal of the Corporation this _____ day of _____ A.D. 190_

_____ Secretary.   _____ President.

This is a stock certificate for one of the 50-odd mining companies that took their living from the Shield around Cobalt. Within ten years Cobalt produced $300 million in metals and led to gold discoveries in the district. The main mining organizations to emerge from the excitement were Dome, Hollinger, and McIntyre.

The Pick of the Crop

Canada's Pride Apples and Canada First Peas, Fleur de Lis Lawton Berries and Horse Shoe Faultless Tomatoes. . .Tinned goods topped the city housewife's shopping list, and the range of produce seemed limitless. From the fertile valleys and farming regions of the country the pick of the crop made its way to processing plants and canneries where any of a dozen different labels like these guaranteed "satisfaction or your money back." Frozen foods were unheard of, and each label bore the message "remove contents of can as soon as opened," a precaution against botulism. (For a view of the inside of a grocery store see page 13.)

90

The June Bug, *built by Alexander Graham Bell's Aerial Experiment Association, is on record as the first airplane to fly one kilometre in the western hemisphere.*

CHAPTER EIGHT

Dr. Bell and the Birdmen

Of course, the Wrights had been flying earlier, only we did not know what they had been doing, as it was all done in private.

Alexander Graham Bell

December 6, 1907, was raw and cold. The Bras d'Or Lakes were as grey as the Cape Breton sky. From the hillside the villagers watched the *Blue Hill* towing the barge with the kite on it, the same sort of kite, red silk and wood, they had seen in the sky so often. Still they waited, stamping their feet. Today was different. Dr. Bell had said that a man would fly today.

Alexander Graham Bell, the inventor of the telephone, had been flying kites at his summer home at Baddeck in Cape Breton for eleven years. But though Bell was rich, and so famous that his mansion at Baddeck was a mecca for the scientific elite, no one seemed to share his belief that flight was possible. His sole converts were the four young men who were helping him stage today's kite flight, a group called the Aerial Experiment Association.

The five of them had come together in this obscure little village by chance. In 1885 Bell had been strolling through town on a holiday, and through the newspaper office window he saw a man struggling with a telephone. Bell walked in. "What's the trouble?"

The editor, Arthur McCurdy, contained his surprise. "I can't imagine what's got into it." Phones were new, still imbued with magic. "And there's probably not a man this side of Halifax can fix it."

Bell asked if he could look at the instrument. McCurdy surrendered it with misgivings. Bell listened briefly, unscrewed the mouthpiece, flicked out a dead fly, and put the phone back together. "It will work now," he said, and explained who he was.

Thus began a lifetime friendship. Bell came up every summer from Washington, a big, bearded man whose energy overflowed in Scottish songs, piano sonatas and histrionic gestures. He built up a 1,600-acre estate he called Beinn Bhreagh (Gaelic for "beautiful mountain") and staffed a laboratory in which he spent more and more time. He hired McCurdy as his secretary, and McCurdy's youngest son, Douglas, grew up with Bell's two daughters.

Douglas was ten in 1896, just old enough to help, when Bell began his experiments with kites. Bell had watched his friend Sam Langley, secretary of the Smithsonian Institute in Washington, fly a steam-powered model plane that year. "The sight," Bell said, "convinced me that the age of the flying machine was at hand." He gave Langley $5,000 and persuaded the American War Department to grant him another $50,000 to build a full-sized machine. But in December 1903, the same

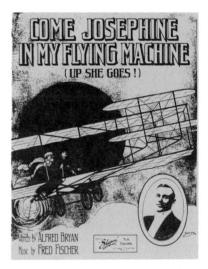

This hit song put an end to Alfred Bryan's years of disappointment and poverty, and lauched him on a long and prolific song-writing career. Bryan grew up in London, Ontario.

Casey Baldwin
The First Canadian Flyer

On March 12, 1908, F.W. Baldwin became the first Canadian to fly an airplane, at Hammondsport, N.Y. He was born in Toronto in 1882 and got his nickname from his illustrious days with the University of Toronto baseball team. An engineering grad, he began flying mainly to prove the worth of planes he helped to design and build at Bell's Aerial Experiment Association from 1907-1909. When the group disbanded, Baldwin tried in vain to interest the army in military uses of airplanes, but the brass was not impressed when two demonstration flights failed at Petawawa. In 1911 he rejoined Bell at Baddeck, N.S., gave up flying and turned his attention to developing hydrofoil watercraft and refining aerodynamic principles.

month that Wilbur and Orville Wright made their historic secret flight in North Carolina, Langley's launching mechanism jammed and dropped his plane into the Potomac River. Langley was labelled a lunatic by the newspapers, "which," said Bell, "effectually prevented Professor Langley from securing further financial aid and, indeed, broke his heart." Langley died three years later.

the dollars dried up

Following this fiasco no organization on the continent would put up a dollar for aviation. The last word on the subject had been pronounced by Simon Newcomb, the world-renowned Canadian astronomer: "An aerial vehicle which could carry even a single man from place to place at pleasure requires the discovery of some new metal or some new force." Bell was risking his reputation, and the eminent scientist Lord Kelvin tried to dissuade him "from giving his valuable time and resources" to experiments that "could only lead to disappointment."

Bell, though liked, was viewed askance in Baddeck. In 1901 his boatman, Angus MacAngus, told an American newspaperman:

He's the queerest man . . . He sets up a blackboard on the hill there – you can see it most any day – and he marks down figures about these kites . . . He must have fifty of them in all kinds of queer shapes . . . It's the greatest nonsense I ever seen in all my life.

By 1906 Bell was building kites so big they were hauled by horses and launched by a horse running down a hill. The McCurdys were now in Toronto. Douglas was twenty, an engineering student. He was packing his clothes at the end of the term to go back to work in Bell's lab when Casey Baldwin wandered into his room.

F. W. "Casey" Baldwin, twenty-four, grandson of an Upper Canada premier, Robert Baldwin,

was one of Canada's best-known athletes, the Varsity football captain and a graduate engineer. McCurdy recalled that Mrs. Bell had often asked him to bring down "another bright young man." He had forgotten about it till now. "Casey," he said, "where are you spending the summer?"

Casey shrugged. He had no job offers.

"Come to Baddeck with me," McCurdy urged.

With nothing better to do, Baldwin agreed to go for two weeks.

He stayed for forty years; Bell took to him immediately. They went out daily that summer and the next, towing kites on pontoons with the motorboat, the young men using spring balances and levels to measure pulls. They brought method to Bell's haphazard work, and enlivened him with their enthusiasm.

Bell now needed power for his kites and the best light engine on the continent was made by Glenn Curtiss of Hammondsport, New York, a twenty-nine-year-old motorcycle maker who had driven the world's fastest mile. Curtiss was not interested in flight; Bell had to pay him to visit Baddeck. Once there, however, the challenge intrigued him.

Roosevelt listened

Bell also wanted official recognition. He called on President Theodore Roosevelt, who assigned him an observer, Thomas Selfridge, a West Point lieutenant with the first U.S. Field Artillery. Selfridge, at twenty-five, had studied all phases of flight, even Wallace Turnbull's first wind-tunnel tests of airfoil models at Rothesay, New Brunswick. He joined eagerly in the work and the evening conversations around the fire in Dr. Bell's big living room.

Bell's wife, Mabel, daughter of his first backer, was deaf, and a very keen observer. One drizzly September night she came into the living room with hot coffee, watched them talking for a few minutes, then said: "Alec, you have four pretty smart young engineers here, and they're just as interested in flight as you are. Why don't we form an organization?" She had just sold some land and would back them with $20,000.

Bell went upstairs to lie down and think about it. In an hour he came down, excited by the prospect. The following month he took the four young men to Halifax and ceremoniously registered the Aerial Experiment Association.

titles meant little

The aim of AEA was "to get a man into the air," for although men had flown development was stalled. Bell was chairman – "his happiest role," one of his biographers, Catherine Mackenzie writes. "A master surrounded by his pupils." Curtiss was director of experiments at a salary of $5,000; Baldwin was chief engineer and McCurdy was treasurer, each at $1,000. Selfridge, an observer on army pay, was secretary. The titles meant little. None of the young men was self-seeking. They lived in Bell's house, sharing the work and risk without rivalry. By December 7 the AEA's first kite was ready to fly.

The Cygnet I was 425 feet across and it looked like a slice of honeycomb. It lay on a barge in the bay, and from the hillside above the villagers watched as the steamer *Blue Hill* approached and dropped a line. The line was fastened to the kite. A man in oilskins crawled into the centre hole. The steamer headed into the wind, belching smoke as its steam pressure rose.

At its top speed of twelve knots the kite lifted off the barge, higher, higher. For seven minutes the villagers gawked at a man flying through the air 168 feet above the water. Then evenly, gently, the kite began to fall. On the *Blue Hill* a crewman stood by the kite rope, ready to cut it loose. But as

Alexander Graham Bell sits in front of his experimental kites at the 1904 St. Louis Exhibition. In 1907 Thomas Selfridge was the first to go aloft on one of Bell's huge tetrahedral kites – the Cygnet I.

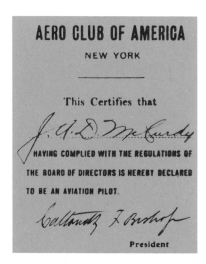

*Pilot's licences testified to skill
and distinction in the early days of
flight, before they became mandatory.
The pioneers held the low numbers:
Glenn Curtiss got No. 1, the Wrights
Nos. 4 and 5, and McCurdy No. 18.*

The Cygnet I settled, his view was blocked by the steamer's smoke.

In his hole in the kite Lieutenant Selfridge was swathed in flapping red silk. He couldn't tell he was dropping; he could see only straight ahead. The kite struck the water but the *Blue Hill* steamed on, ripping the kite to shreds. The smoke lifted. Shouts rang out from the *Blue Hill*. She came about and Selfridge, who had managed somehow to jump clear, was hauled unhurt from the numbing cold water.

first Canadian aloft

The wreck of *The Cygnet I* ended work that year at Baddeck. Bell had business all winter in Washington, so the AEA moved to Hammondsport, where Curtiss had his factory. Among hills well suited to gliding, they applied their knowledge of kites to gliders. With wings fitted over their shoulders they would run downhill, leaping and gliding. When they knew how to keep a glider level in flight they built a biplane, framed in bamboo and covered in red silk left over from *The Cygnet I*. On March 12, 1908, with Bell and Selfridge away in Washington, McCurdy and Curtiss skated out on nearby Lake Keuka pushing the *Red Wing*.

Several hundred watchers had gathered. The Wrights had circled their airfield three years before for thirty-eight minutes in 1905, but few recognized their feat because, to protect their discoveries, they had barred even newspapermen from their field. At a time when the ultimate expression of the impossible was "I could no more do that than fly," the AEA was staging the first public airplane flight in North America.

The day was windless, the ice bare. The *Red Wing* slid smoothly on its sled runners. Behind it came Casey Baldwin, slipping and sliding in his shoes. He had mislaid his skates, so he was to fly; fitting enough, since most of the *Red Wing*'s inno-

vations were his: the tail rudder; the wings tapered like a bird's; and behind the wings a little streamlined enclosure, the first airplane cockpit. Curtiss started his air-cooled motor and the plane took off by itself, McCurdy and Curtiss dashing after it, grabbing at its tail.

They brought it back and held it while Baldwin climbed in. Curtiss gunned the motor. "Let go!" Baldwin shouted. They jumped back.

The plane shot forward, the crowd surging after it. It taxied fifty yards, then lifted up four or five feet. The crowd cheered. For 319 feet the plane swooped above the ice. Then the motor cut out, overheated, and Baldwin bumped down, the first Canadian to fly a plane and the seventh pilot in the world.

front-page news

The flight was front-page news across the continent, with the papers crediting Captain Baldwin, the famous balloonist. The AEA members, though a bit put out, were exhilarated by their triumph. And the New York *Sun* set the record straight with a Sunday feature on them, headed "Man Really About to Fly." Overnight they had changed the climate for aviation.

Five days later Baldwin crashed. "Dear Casey," Bell wrote from Washington, "I am much relieved to know that you escaped from the wreck of the *Red Wing* uninjured. Of course I am glad that the engine escaped too, but I don't wish to put you both in the same sentence." From this crash came Baldwin's concept of the aileron, a hinged wing tip that tilted up or down, the first and still the most important device for achieving stability.

In May they pushed their second machine, the *White Wing*, to the Hammondsport race track on three motorcycle wheels – the first tricycle gear. With large crowds watching and Bell on the sidelines, Baldwin and Selfridge went up separately and were each forced down when wing fabric and loose wire fouled the propeller. Then McCurdy on his first flight raced at such speed down the track that Selfridge had no time to jump clear, and escaped death by dropping flat. McCurdy got up to twenty feet, caught a gust of wind and crashed. For weeks he was walking with a crutch.

Their third plane was the *June Bug*. One morning she failed to lift. Her wings, McCurdy noticed, were heavy with dew. In the big borrowed circus tent that served them as a hangar they mixed paraffin, ochre and gasoline and slapped the mixture on the wings. The *June Bug* flew so well that on June 25 Bell received this wire from Selfridge:

Curtiss flew 1,140 yards in sixty seconds this evening about 7:30. We have telegraphed and telephoned secretary Aero Club of America that we are now ready to try for the Scientific American Cup. Hurray!

fly a straight line

The cup was for the first airplane to fly a kilometre in a straight line, officially measured at Hammondsport on July 4, 1908. On his first try Curtiss was slightly short and the plane was towed back for a second, successful attempt. Bell was still in Washington, but a letter from his daughter, Mrs. David Fairchild, conveyed the excitement:

. . . in spite of all that I had read and heard, and all the photographs I had seen, the actual sight of a man flying through the air was thrilling to a degree that I can't express.

We all lost our heads and shouted and I cried and everybody cheered and clapped, and engines tooted . . . All sorts of pictures were taken, and the air was full of the click, click of shutters . . .

. . . As Mr. Curtiss flew over the red flag which marked the finish and went on his way toward the trees, I don't think any of us quite knew what we were doing.

The AEA's second plane, White Wing, *was fitted with "ailerons" (term coined in 1908). That set off a legal battle with the Wright brothers over patent rights that lasted into WW I.*

Casey Baldwin and J.A.D. McCurdy tried to sell the Canadian army on planes in 1909, with demonstrations at Petawawa, Ont. Baddeck I *(above) and* Silver Dart *both crashed after several flights. No sale.*

**J.A.D. McCurdy
The Flying Stunt Man**

At a time when death was an accepted and common hazard of flying, J.A.D. McCurdy carried on as if he had nine lives. He barnstormed, set distance records, raced and gave stunt-flying exhibitions from Canada to Mexico. McCurdy grew up in Baddeck, N.S., studied engineering at the U of T, and returned home in 1907 to join Alexander Graham Bell's Aerial Experiment Association. There he showed his genius as a designer by producing the *Silver Dart*, the most advanced plane of its time and the first plane to fly in the British Empire when he took it up in Feb. 1909. In the early days of WW I he tried to convince Ottawa of the strategic value of airplanes in war, but Sam Hughes humbugged the idea as "an invention of the devil." Thirty years later the government asked McCurdy, then head of a Montreal aircraft firm, to become director of government aircraft production.

The *June Bug* flew 150 flights or more without mishap. It induced the American Army to test the Wrights' plane that September, and Selfridge was ordered to fly with Orville Wright as an observer. After circling around and around the field Wright crashed with a sheared propeller, fracturing a leg and a hip and breaking five ribs. But Selfridge had run out of luck; he was instantly killed, the first man to meet death in a flying machine.

Gloom enveloped the Hammondsport factory where McCurdy and Curtiss had just built a fourth plane, the *Silver Dart,* a two-seater with the world's first water-cooled aircraft engine. Baldwin had gone to Baddeck to help Bell and from there Mrs. Bell wrote "her boys":

I can't get over Tom's being taken. I can't realize it; it doesn't seem possible. Isn't it heart-breaking? And yet it is better for him than to die as poor Langley did. He was so happy to the very end.

I am so sorry for you in this breaking of your beautiful association. But it was beautiful and the memory of it will endure – Bell, Curtiss, Baldwin, Selfridge and McCurdy. It was indeed a "brilliant coterie," as one newspaper said. Do anything you think best, but let the AEA be only these to the end, and then take some other name.

first hop in Canada

The AEA's year was up in October but Mrs. Bell put up $10,000 to extend it another six months. McCurdy test-flew the *Silver Dart,* then shipped it to Baddeck. On February 23, 1909, it was hauled out on the ice for the first flight of an airplane in Canada.

The entire countryside had turned out; school children had a half-holiday. Everyone knew of the flights in the United States but seeing was believing. McCurdy in a stocking cap tried the engine, the controls. Then he told Bell, huge in a fur coat, that he was ready.

"The doctor isn't here yet," Bell said. He constantly worried about their safety and had hired a doctor to stand by when they were flying. "We'll wait for the doctor."

The doctor arrived, apologizing. McCurdy climbed into the cockpit. Police pushed back the crowd and McCurdy taxied into the wind, rose gracefully to thirty feet, flew three-quarters of a mile, turned and flew back to his starting point, coolly veering to miss two small girls. "Everyone," said the Washington *Star,* "seemed dumbfounded." People threw hats and mitts into the air and cheered wildly. "Now I'll take her up for a real flight," McCurdy said.

at a dizzy height

"No, no," said Bell, talking as much to the crowd as to McCurdy. "What we have seen just now may well prove to be one of the really important pages in history. I wouldn't want it spoiled. Douglas, you can fly her again tomorrow if you like, but that's all for today."

Next day McCurdy crossed the lake at the dizzy height of sixty feet. By March he had flown more than a thousand miles, over houses, over trees, up to twenty miles at a time. Only the Wrights had flown farther and no one had flown more. McCurdy by now was perhaps the most skillful pilot in the world.

On March 31, at midnight, the AEA dissolved. Curtiss went back to Hammondsport to make aircraft engines. Baldwin and McCurdy formed the Canadian Aerodrome Company. With Bell's backing they put together two planes at Baddeck, developing the first enclosed gas tanks and the first wing radiators.

Bell was still stubbornly trying to fly his great motorized kites –a failure that does not detract from his role as the leading midwife of flight. Even before the Wrights had flown in 1903 he had written: "I fully expect to live to see the day when a man can take dinner in New York and breakfast the next morning in Liverpool." He gave reporters 25-cent cigars and such newsworthy statements as "The nation that controls the air will ultimately rule the world." He had badgered Theodore Roosevelt into honouring the Wrights in 1908. In 1909 he made a speech in Ottawa on behalf of his two young Canadian colleagues.

At Bell's invitation the governor general, Lord Grey, spent a week at Baddeck and, standing in a meadow in the rain, watched McCurdy fly. "Extraordinary," said His Excellency. "Extraordinary. How like a bird!" And the army finally agreed to a demonstration at Petawawa.

On the morning of August 2, McCurdy flew the *Silver Dart* fifty feet above the general staff at fifty miles an hour. He demonstrated turns, four successful takeoffs and landings. But on his fifth landing his wheels hit sand and sunk in. The plane nosed over. McCurdy was pulled from the wreck with a broken nose.

"nays have it"

Baldwin, who had been mingling with the officers on the ground, came over and said, "The nays have it." The fifth flight was declared the official flight and labelled a failure, ending the brief history of Canada's first aircraft company. Baldwin took over Bell's lab.

McCurdy went barnstorming. He put on air shows from race tracks across the continent, gradually rising to 2,500 feet. "I sometimes think we were crazy," he said later. "Some of the fields were so short, in fact, that we used to have two men, each holding one end of a long rope stretched across the field, so that when we landed the machine would run into the rope and bring us to a stop before we hit the fence."

In 1910 at Lakeside Park near Montreal McCurdy staged the first air meet in Canada. In that same year he was the first to demonstrate bombing from the air, dropping oranges with great precision onto a "battleship" of white cloth. He was the first man to fly in Cuba, the first to fly in Mexico, the first (in 1911) to use wireless in a plane. His flight from Key West to Havana that year set a new overseas record and made him a hero, the Lindbergh of his day.

Baldwin became Bell's indispensable right hand. And while trying to get Bell's unflyable kites on pontoons into the air, he developed a boat with submerged blades, a hydroplane or sea sled, and later built the first torpedo boat.

first airplane factory

Curtiss, who had set up the first American aircraft factory, went on to conceive the aircraft carrier in 1910, fitting a wooden landing deck on the American cruiser *Birmingham*. He would later build the first practical seaplane, the first flying boat, and design the first engines for military aircraft and dirigibles.

It had all come out of a chance meeting at Baddeck. The Aerial Experiment Association had lasted only eighteen months, but it had put four machines into the air and made the first public flights; invented the aileron, wing dope and tricycle landing gear; developed the cockpit, enclosed gas tanks and wing radiators; and adapted the water-cooled engine to an aircraft. Most important, it had shown North Americans that man could fly, at a time when faith in aviation was at its weakest.

The generous impulse of Mabel Bell had been a fortuitous incident. Five kindred spirits had met and she had set them a goal. She had held them together briefly for an adventure, almost a lark, in which the life's course of each had altered with far-reaching consequences.

**William Wallace Gibson
The Unknown Aviator**

W.W. Gibson was a gutsy, determined pioneer of aviation. Working alone much of the time in a society of scoffers, and often out of money, he achieved impressive results. He moved from Saskatchewan to Victoria B.C., in 1906 with plans for an airplane engine. It was a failure, but his second in 1910, was the first successful aircraft engine made in Canada. The maiden flight of his first airplane, the "Twin-plane," in 1910, was the first free flight by a Canadian-built plane. But since Gibson avoided publicity few knew of his flights; recognition followed far behind. Finding himself out of money after the crash of his second plane in 1911, and with a family to support, Gibson gave up flying for good. But his work was not in vain; many modern airplanes have used ideas pioneered by Gibson in 1911, when his sceptical neighbours, meeting him in the street, would flap their arms, wing-like, in derision.

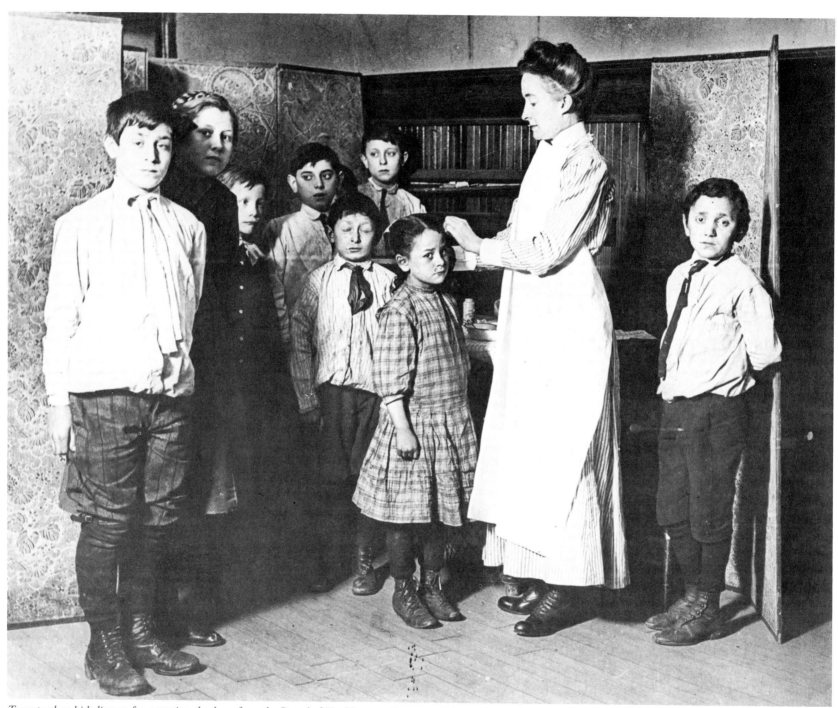

Toronto slum kids line up for a routine check-up from the Board of Health nurse. Poverty and disease have left their mark; there's not a clean shirt in this group.

CHAPTER NINE

"Strangers Within Our Gates"

To really save one man you must transform the community in which he lives.

J. S. Woodsworth

The infant lies on a table at one end of the room. It is clothed in white. The table is decorated with flowers – not real ones, just paper and wool. Three beer bottles serve as candle-holders at the child's head; a loaf of bread with a hole in the top holds another candle at the feet. There is no priest here because the parents are too poor. A singer from their church leads the funeral service. A few friends and neighbours have crowded into this single room they live in.

When the service ends the undertaker is supposed to remove the body and bury it. First, though, he draws the parents aside to tell them he has orders to collect the funeral expenses before removing the body.

Everyone knows the parents have no money. Someone had notified the city of the death and asked it to bear the expense of the burial. Well, yes, the city normally buries paupers for free. But when an investigator came to visit the family he found a freshly-opened keg of beer and several drunken people in the room. The family could afford beer, so it could afford to pay.

The neighbours intervene. These people really are poor; neither is well enough to work. Friends have paid all their costs so far, even supplying the beer. But they can't afford to pay any more. What is to be done? The mother's cries of anguish are heart-breaking.

It is finally too much for the undertaker. He says he will bear the expense himself if he cannot collect from the city. He takes the body and leaves.

* * *

That was death somewhere in Winnipeg's "Foreign Quarter," the North End, literally the other side of the CPR tracks. The incident would never be reported in the papers and the parents' names would never be known. Most Canadians wouldn't have been able to pronounce the names anyway, let alone spell them. Even the canvassers making the listings for *Henderson's City Directory* simply gave up and used the catch-all designation, "foreigner."

There were mostly foreigners in the North End by 1910 and most of them were poor. Jacob Lalucki, a Ruthenian who worked in the CPR shops, lived there with his Polish wife and two children in one room. Michael Yakoff and his wife had three rooms, but they paid $8 a month rent from Michael's $12 earnings as a caretaker. The Yakoffs took in roomers, and little Pieter Yakoff, age eight, brought in a few pennies scavenging for wood in North End alleys. He never went to school.

Almost everyone took in roomers. Fifteen to

J.S. Woodsworth's concern over the troubles of immigrants in Canada led him to write his pioneer sociological study, Strangers within our Gates.

John Kelso stands with three wards of the Children's Aid Society. Kelso pioneered systems for the protection of neglected delinquent children in Ontario, and was a guiding hand in many organizations like the Children's Fresh Air Fund. He was the main force behind passage of the Children's Protection Act of 1893, under which he set up Children's Aid Societies.

twenty men slept in Peter Yabroof's two rented rooms, the same number in the four rooms where John Klenbyel lived with his wife and six children. Immigrants poured into the city and had to have shelter. In their boarding house at 37 Austin Street, the Kozuchars crowded twenty-five people, men and women together, into three rooms. Mrs. Chudek, proprietor of 47 Austin Street, had thirty-two people in rooms that might sleep seven. She was taken to court and lectured by the magistrate: *People are supposed to live like human beings and not like hogs. In your house there was not space for a dog, let alone a man. Besides being overcrowded the place was abominably filthy and as a starter I'll fine you twenty dollars and costs.*

a brisk business

The houses on Annabella and McFarlane Street took in more customers but turned them out again more quickly. In two and a half hours one night 292 men were counted going in and out of fourteen of the Annabella Street residences. Minnie Woods, Lulu Thornton, Lila Anderson, Gertie Curney – there was no trouble pronouncing the names of the ladies who owned these properties in Winnipeg's "red light" district. There were not any red lights actually, just the brightest electric porch lights in town and foot-high house numbers.

Of course, respectable Winnipegers moved out of the North End almost as fast as the immigrants and the madames moved in. To WASP Winnipeg, the North End was a giant melting-pot-of-a-slum, "a howling chaos . . . an endless grey expanse of mouldering ruin, a heap seething with unwashed children, sick men in grey underwear, vast sweating women in vaster petticoats." In his popular 1909 novel, *The Foreigner,* Ralph Connor contrasted "respectable Winnipeg . . . snugly asleep under snow-covered roofs and smoking chimneys," with the "sordid drunken dance and song . . . sanguinary fighting . . . nauseating spectacle" of a wedding celebration in the North End.

tried to resign

The Woodsworth family, eminently respectable and unquestionably Canadian, lived in the North End by choice. The Reverend James Shaver Woodsworth, only in his thirties, was already richly experienced as a Methodist clergyman. He had conducted revival meetings in country churches, preached on "The Sin of Indifference" to Winnipeg's wealthiest Methodists at Grace Church, ministered to lumberjacks and railwaymen in British Columbia and been a circuit rider on the prairies. He had twice tried to resign from the ministry. He no longer believed in miracles, the virgin birth, original sin, the need for personal conversion. The Manitoba Conference had refused to accept his resignation. The desire to serve, the Church's more enlightened ministers believed, was more important than rigid adherence to inflexible points of doctrine. They persuaded Woodsworth to try a new kind of Christian service as superintendent of All Peoples' Mission.

All Peoples' Mission had grown out of the Sunday School classes Dolly McGuire held in the 1890s for foreign children she collected from the streets. It now had ten buildings in the North End, a staff of twenty-three and over a hundred part-time volunteers. It ministered to Poles, Jews, Ruthenians, Galicians, Swedes, Germans, anyone who chose to come.

At All Peoples' North Enders learned English, attended kindergarten (there was none in the public schools), took housekeeping classes, borrowed books, got food and clothing in emergencies, worshipped in their native languages, joined the Ruthenian Temperance Society, the Bohemian Club, the Boy Scouts. It was good of the nice young ladies from the Mission to visit little Lader Doerchuch last year when the train ran over his leg and it had to be amputated. Dunka and Nastaoma Ladowska are doing well in the kindergarten, but no one is quite sure how to help their mother keep their father, a cruel man, away from the family. The older Klenbyel girl won't live at home because of the dirt and drunkenness.

purest idealism

Coping with the misery and poverty of the North End was at once depressing and exhilarating. The chaste, prim deaconesses and the chaste, proper theology students from Wesley College were appalled that such conditions existed in twentieth century Canada. But it did give them the chance to save bodies as well as souls and to take Christ to the poor, the oppressed, the stranger.

> *Seek those of evil behaviour,*
> *Bid them their lives to amend;*
> *Go, point the lost world to the Saviour,*
> *And be to the friendless a friend.*
> *Still be the lone heart of anguish*
> *Soothed by the pity of thine;*
> *By waysides, if wounded ones languish,*
> *Go, pour in the oil and the wine.*

The Christian activists at All Peoples' were nothing if not sincere. Theirs was this decade's purest idealism, a belief that the Christian's highest calling was to do good to fellow humans.

Some of their suggestions for improving Canadian society were very much a product of their time and place. Woodsworth, for example, wrote that "every city or community ought to maintain a strict censorship by which all immoral or debasing pictures could be absolutely prohibited." He feared that the revolutionary new moving picture would undermine family life. He worried, too, about the "octopus of Mormonism," stretching its

Church photographers caught child labourers in Toronto (above), and a Polish slum in North End Winnipeg (below). The Protestant churches saw their duty in social concern on "the other side of the tracks."

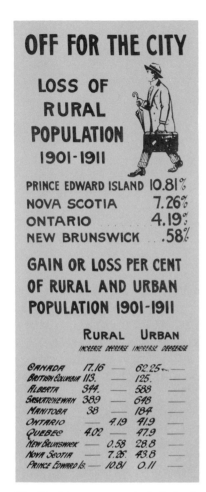

OFF FOR THE CITY

LOSS OF RURAL POPULATION 1901-1911

PRINCE EDWARD ISLAND	10.81%
NOVA SCOTIA	7.26%
ONTARIO	4.19%
NEW BRUNSWICK	.58%

GAIN OR LOSS PER CENT OF RURAL AND URBAN POPULATION 1901-1911

	RURAL		URBAN	
	INCREASE	DECREASE	INCREASE	DECREASE
CANADA	17.16	—	62.25	—
BRITISH COLUMBIA	113.	—	125.	—
ALBERTA	344.	—	588.	—
SASKATCHEWAN	389	—	648	—
MANITOBA	38	—	184	—
ONTARIO	—	4.19	41.9	—
QUEBEC	4.02	—	47.9	—
NEW BRUNSWICK	—	0.58	28.8	—
NOVA SCOTIA	—	7.26	43.8	—
PRINCE EDWARD IS.	—	10.81	0.11	—

The Maritimes were particularly hard hit by the steady trickle of people to the cities. By the mid-1920s, city-dwellers outnumbered country folk.

J.S. Woodsworth (centre-left, middle row) and this group of socially concerned and active church members tackled the serious social problems resulting from crowded cities, poverty, illiteracy and industrialization, in Winnipeg's immigrant neighbourhoods.

polygamous tentacles from Utah into Canada via Alberta. He believed in prohibition. He believed that the Chinese ought to be excluded from Canada because they would never fit in. Like most missionaries, he started his work with a vague idea of turning his charges into sober, industrious, grace-saying Protestant Canadians.

Woodsworth was too earnest to be colourful. "He has no sense of humour – he really doesn't," one reporter had noted. In his spare time he studied the literature of social reform, trying to see how the spirit of All Peoples' could be translated into wider service. "Preventive rather than remedial measures are necessary to social progress," he wrote in one report; and in another, "In future the work must be . . . more extensive in bringing about such changes in our social system as will enable men and women and little children to live out their highest lives."

His most important work at the Mission was simple publicizing. He averaged a hundred speeches a year across Canada and in the United States describing the need for missions to the forgotten foreigners in the cities. In 1909 he published *Strangers Within Our Gates* and in 1911 *My Neighbor,* to warn Canadians of the seamy side of immigration and urban growth. His books were studied by Methodist young people across the country and All Peoples' itself became a training ground for a generation of Manitoba social workers and reformers, including Nellie McClung.

The country needed dedicated social workers. The North End in Winnipeg, The Ward in Toronto, Germantown in Regina, Chinatown in Vancouver – in every major city immigration and rapid urban growth had created ghettos where the desperately poor huddled together under leaking roofs in ramshackle frame houses for a few cents a

Churches circulated posters like this one to twig society's conscience. The Anglo-Saxon view was to help, then assimilate, the immigrants.

This is a kindergarten class at All Peoples' Mission, which used trained teachers at a time when Winnipeg had no kindergarten classes at all. All Peoples' also arranged fresh-air camps and medical care for sick children, and English classes for adults.

night. Edmonton was an exception – there they slept in tents because there weren't enough houses. A doctor reported that this was healthier than living in slum rooming houses.

Many immigrants arrived on the prairies at the wrong time of the year; others had no money to start homesteading; others did not know how to farm or could not bear the loneliness. Thousands flocked back to the cities every winter when the railway camps closed down.

The young and healthy found jobs in slaughterhouses and sweatshops, worked as laundresses and cleaning ladies. They laid track on the frontier, dug ditches and put in sewers in the cities. The old and sick and widowed survived as best they could, or simply didn't. Even in the best of times, as these were – it was a strange, hard country to make your way in.

The old Canadians welcomed immigrants as workers, but were not sure what they thought of these strangers as human beings. The newspapers and magazines supported "Canadianizing" the immigrant, but the stock of goodwill went only so far. In 1909, for example, the *Canadian Courier* (Canada's first national newsmagazine) printed without comment a long letter suggesting that missionaries working with Canada's Chinese were going about things the wrong way: "Withdraw the pretty teacher, and if the Chink must be converted allee samee, place his conversion in the hands of men of strength, courage and determination enough to teach him Christianity with a baseball bat . . ." The Chinese were "Chinks" who smoked opium and robbed graves; the Italians were "dagos" who carried knives; the Slavs were "bohunks" who were dumb and lousy.

Prejudice and ignorance notwithstanding, it was an active decade for reformers like Woods-

A motor-oil crate and patch of ground are the setting for an impromptu concert that captivates seven small passers-by. Money wasn't everything to this tattered fiddler.

worth. A wealthy country advancing proudly into the twentieth century *could* be saved from the worst social problems of the Old World. J.J. Kelso had become nationally prominent for his work with neglected children. Dr. Charles Hastings became Hogtown's first crusading public health officer. Quebec factory inspectors Louis Guyon and Louise Provencher carried on a dogged campaign against child labour. Working for the Presbyterian Church, Sara Libby Carson helped found settlement houses in downtown areas across the country. Margaret Scott's Nursing Mission complemented the work of All Peoples' in Winnipeg, and the Salvation Army's Adjutant McElhaney specialized in redeeming the fallen women of Annabella and McFarlane Streets.

immigrants neglected

The Reverend Alfred Fitzpatrick realized that immigrant workers on the frontier were the most neglected of all. In 1901 he founded the Canadian Reading Camp Association, later to become Frontier College, to bring education to the men in the shanties and bunkhouses. In the theological colleges men like Salem Bland were preaching that Christ's message was a social gospel, designed to save society now, not souls for Heaven later. Fitzpatrick, Woodsworth, Bland and the other social gospellers were giving Canadian churches a vital role to play in what otherwise might have been a secular century.

There were more dimensions to urban blight than ghettos and overcrowding, however. The streets of every Canadian city were a tangle of streetcar tracks and wires, telephone poles and wires, electricity poles and wires. Most city councils were locked in perpetual battles with the private street railway, telephone and electricity companies over rights-of-way, service and rates. Middle-class city dwellers wanted an end to the ty-

The desperation of this homeless group is almost tangible. Resistance to immigration grew in Canada as the number of destitute foreigners increased in city tenements, jails , and on street curbs.

Poverty was not limited to the newest Canadians. For these women and urchins the life on the reserves held little opportunity: hand-me-down white-men's clothes are worn by everybody.

**Adam Beck
The Power Behind Power**

He was feared, hated, idolized and branded a socialist, but before he died in 1925, Adam Beck had made good his promise that even "the poorest working man will have light in his home." It was a mystery why Beck, a wealthy cigar-box maker from Baden, Ont., should lead the fight against power-barons like William Mackenzie, Donald Mann and Henry Pellatt, who controlled Ontario's hydro-electric utilities. In the 1905 election, the ownership of power was a major issue, and the Liberals were swept out of office. A year later Premier Whitney set up the Hydro Commission with Beck as chairman; the struggle was on to put power in the hands of a publicly-owned company. It took four years for the first town to be lit up (Berlin, Ont.), and years of dirty political battles before the private interests were beaten, but by 1917 Beck controlled the world's largest public power commission.

phoid epidemics caused by polluted water supplies and the lung ailments brought on by breathing coal dust all winter. A few of them wanted parks and playgrounds for the poor.

By the end of the decade urban reform had become almost as popular a cause as prohibition. The heir to a tannery, Morley Wickett, had written the first Canadian text on municipal government. A former *Bleu* journalist and provincial cabinet minister, G.A. Nantel, had proposed a grandiose scheme of civic betterment for Montreal in *La Métropole de Demain*. In Guelph and Port Arthur, Ottawa and Moncton, cities were successfully running their own public utilities. W.D. Lighthall, the reform mayor of Westmount, had helped found the Canadian Union of Municipalities to fight grasping utility companies. Manitoba had bought out the province's fledgling telephone system and was offering telephone service as a *public* utility. Laurier's postmaster-general, William Mulock, had wanted to offer the same service nationally through his department. Perhaps it was just as well that he failed – but the telephone was never closer to being nationalized than it was in 1906.

beat the corporations

In Ontario Adam Beck did win his battle against the corporations. On October 11, 1910, Conservative Premier J.P. Whitney pressed Beck's hand against a button in the Berlin, Ontario, skating rink and a little girl's tiara of electric light bulbs lit up. It was the birth of the world's first publicly-owned hydroelectric company. The *Financial Post* wailed that Ontario's "socialist" premier had abolished the Magna Carta in his fight to establish "The People's Power." It was not often noticed that the "people" who had shouted the loudest for public power were manufacturers, like Adam Beck, out after the lowest possible rates.

As the hydro fight showed, reformers were most successful when their schemes benefitted the middle and upper classes. There were a handful of doctrinaire socialists in the country, but no one in power seriously talked about income redistribution, the welfare state, or even income taxes. Woodsworth himself was just taking the first steps on his road to socialism and the CCF.

moulded by courage

The greatest resource that reformers could draw on to shape the future had nothing to do with their ideology or the institutions they set up or the laws they had passed. The future was really going to be moulded by the strength and courage and cultural values of ordinary Canadians, the new Canadians as well as the old. Were the foreigners and their strange customs actually a threat to Canadian ideals? Go back to Winnipeg in 1910 and consider one of those foreign weddings Ralph Connor wrote about so critically.

The groom is a packing-house worker, the bride a maid in a hotel. Both are from Poland. They have not learned English and they have not become Protestants. They celebrate their marriage with most undignified dancing, feasting, and much too much beer and wine. But as their celebration comes to an end, listen – if you can understand it – to the advice the young couple is given by the patriarch in his formal "Declamation":

Life is not all music and dancing; there will be the dark side too; there must be toil and weariness, but be true to the best of the Old Land and the New. If children are granted you, shield them, be patient with them, teach them, that they may be a helpful example to others.

After their wedding trip – if they have been able to afford one – the young Polish-Canadian couple will settle down to working and raising a family in the North End.

Fraternal Orders

The Independent Order of Foresters was just one of many benevolent societies brought to Canada in the 19th century–Masons, Elks, Odd-Fellows. They raised funds for charity, organized help for the poor and generally revealed strong social consciences. They also arranged insurance and fellowship for members. Some, like the Knights of Columbus and the Orange Lodge of British America, met mainly for religious reasons. Oronhyatheka (above), Mohawk chief from Brampton, Ont., and a graduate of Oxford University, was the IOF's Supreme Chief Ranger from 1881 until his death in 1907. This picture of him appeared on one of many IOF badges.

The Season's Fancies C.O.D.

The most popular book in Canada, some said. Predictable as the snowfall, the new Eaton's catalogue arrived at the door to announce the change of season. Families settled down to loving study and discussion of the Cyclone Senior plate camera or the latest in hats. And when the orders were sent out, and after the next issue arrived, the old catalogue found its last rest near a well-used, private seat of honour "out back" for re-cycling or reading.

The catalogues gave people things to dream about – like a $125 coat.

All riding equipment, except horses, could be ordered from the catalogue.

Pictures of campers, fishermen, and languid ladies in hammocks were calculated to perk up summer sales.

Is it me, my outfit, or the new lamp on my bicycle that she fell for? The ingredients of charm were available C.O.D.

Business tried to get a foot in the door with colourful and friendly-sounding brochures. The next-door-neighbours' names found in this promotional pamphlet from Dr. Williams' Medicine Co. in Brockville, Ont., testified that no matter what ailed you, you would be cured by "pink pills for pale people."

CHAPTER TEN

Kings of Commerce

*Call it capitalism if you like and kick it.
But it is all we've got.*

Stephen Leacock

When the world-wide depression ended in 1896, Canadian business started to boom. By 1901 trade was growing faster in Canada than anywhere in the world and money was pouring into the country from the United States and Britain. Visitors claimed they could feel the excitement of growth in the air.

The Canadian Locomotive Company was building the world's biggest engines for the world's biggest railway, the CPR. P.C. Larkin of Toronto's Salada Tea Company was the "Tea King of America." Casavant Frères of St. Hyacinthe was the most renowned name in organs. Nordheimer and Heintzman were shipping Toronto pianos to Europe for such customers as Luisa Tetrazzini and Enrico Caruso. MacLaren's cheese was selling in China, Malpeque oysters were tops on the continent, and Manitoba wheat took first prize at the 1901 Pan-American Exposition. Calgary's Pat Burns had meat-packing plants in London and Yokohama, and Walter Massey was selling "Made in Canada" machinery around the world.

A 1901 *Munsey's Magazine* article described the "up-to-date businessman" as one who extended his voice with a telephone, his memory with a card-index, his sales staff with a mail-order system and his energy with a typist. The new flat-top desk stood for "definite clear-cut thinking."

A job-seeker with an economics degree would not usually admit it for fear of being turned down as a "theorist." The only sound school, many businessmen claimed, was the school of hard knocks. Nine phrenologists in Toronto and four in Montreal made a lucrative living helping businessmen to pick employees and assisting young men to pick careers by reading the bumps on their heads, which indicated their mental and moral capacities.

The nearest thing to a national magazine was named, naturally, *Busy Man's.* In 1905 it was writing about "the science of selling goods," but its ads were unsophisticated. The Pollock Cabinet Talking Machine was "the first to get rid of the horn." The Elliott-Fisher Machine had "the ability to write, figure and add . . . with unerring accuracy *in one operation.*" The thermos was "a luxury that the world has never known before." Patent medicines were a cure-all and soap claimed only to clean.

Busy Man's was a genteel apologist for the rich. "The contrast, so commonly drawn, between the millionaire as a man suffocated with wealth and luxury and his employees as having nothing but their incomes is utterly fallacious," wrote Adam Shortt, a Queen's University economist. "A man might be a multi-millionaire in Grand Trunk ordinary stock and yet not enjoy an income from it

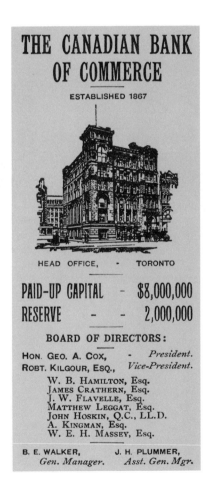

This page from a Commerce passbook assured customers that their savings were in capable hands and that many other people stored their money here.

**Pat Burns
Calgary's Cattle King**

From New York to Yokohama, he was known as "The Cattle King of the British North-West." Pat Burns set up his firm in Calgary in 1890, 12 years after moving west from his home town, Oshawa, Ont., and in no time built a meat-packing empire that spanned the continents, with plants from England to Japan. When western ranchers wanted a good price for their beef, Burns outbid the competition. Guy Weadick needed backing for the Stampede; Burns was one of the men who put up the money. Under his friendly smile and jovial manner he was a hard-nosed business man. On more than one occasion, he refused nomination as a candidate for federal politics but served in the Senate for five years before he died. By then he had made a million many times over.

Behind the scenes at Pat Burns' meat-packing plant in Calgary the boss, in derby and overcoat, casts a critical eye over the red brand beef and poultry hanging in cold storage. Burns built his meat-packing firm into one of the world's largest.

equal to that of a common section man on the road." For these poverty-stricken millionaires *Busy Man's* ran such articles as "How to Foster Habits of Economy and Self-Denial."

It was the age of the magnate, a time when great fortunes were spawned, a time before consultants, committees, or diffusion of decision-making power. A time when men owned the companies they managed, proud, self-willed men, aggressive in action, isolate in thought. They believed in physical change but philosophers long defunct had fixed their beliefs in the nineteenth century. Adam Smith's doctrine of laissez-faire and Charles Darwin's "survival of the fittest" had been blended in the philosophy of Herbert Spencer: "The entire industrial organization in all its marvellous complexity has risen from the pursuit by each person of his own interest."

Lester Patrick, the most famous of the first hockey pros, expressed the beliefs of most businessmen in describing turn-of-the-century shinny as "a wild melee of kids battling a puck around, with no rules, no organization, nothing but individual effort to grab and hold the puck." The businessmen, like the boys, were on their own, looking out for themselves.

The decade "witnessed more money-making," the American *Review of Reviews* announced, "than any other in history." Sir Henry Pellatt, who was reported to have made $17 million in Toronto electric utilities and Cobalt mining stocks, drew up plans in 1910 for Casa Loma, the most palatial residence in North America. It was to have fifty rooms, thirty bathrooms, twenty-five fireplaces, three bowling alleys, fifty-two phones, and the world's finest indoor rifle range. The stable alone, with its Spanish mahogany stalls and Persian rugs, would cost Sir Henry $250,000.

Clerks and accountants at the Proteau & Carignan brewery offices in Quebec City hunch over their hardwood desks. Note the 1909 telephone in foreground and the calendar on the wall–in English. An apprentice (left) sits in on the day's work.

Henry Pellatt
Last of the Big-Time Spenders

Henry Pellatt's legacy has been called half 19th-century Gothic and half 20th-century Fox. A flamboyant spender, he sank $2 million into the building of Casa Loma (the "castle" contains 98 rooms plus 30 bathrooms); he once had a set of custom false teeth made for his favourite horse; and in 1910 he took the entire 620 men of the Queen's Own Rifles to England to review British Army manoeuvres at his own expense. He was born in Toronto in 1860 and began his career as a financier and stock-broker.When Niagara power promised him a fortune, he organized the Toronto Electric Light Company and cornered a substantial part of the city's electrical sources until the Hydro Act of 1906 brought the utility under public control. Pellatt lost his fortune in the '29 crash: even the monument he built to himself, Casa Loma, was taken for back taxes.

Business helped maintain morality. In Toronto, which boasted more piety per foot of downtown frontage than any city on the continent, the T. Eaton company refused to sell playing cards, the *Toronto Star* refused whisky ads, and the *Globe* would not advertise sanitary napkins. Most papers supported the temperance movement, growing fast in reaction to frontier indulgence, and opposed the wearing of bloomers by women.

Government was simple, unions were weak and the poor had little protection from the law. People in trouble had to rely on their own abilities, and few thought of opposing the causes of common evils. Journalists who called for reform were "muck-rakers" and rare; most editors were businessmen with views akin to their business colleagues.

The creed of the day was "God helps those who help themselves." The American Horatio Al-ger had planted it in the brains of businessmen from the Rio Grande to Hudson Bay. Alger had died in 1899 after writing seventy-odd books – or as someone said one book seventy-odd times – in which a poor boy rose to riches by hard work, thrift, and shrewdness. The fruit of virtue was wealth, so to be wealthy was to be virtuous. Similarly, to be poor was to be lazy, wasteful or stupid.

To some millionaires, the inevitability of progress suggested divine purpose; if a man became rich it was clearly God's design. An income tax would therefore have been a transgression of God's will, a shareholder's report a violation of His economic law.

By decade's end, however, some elements in the society were tiring of rampant individualism and unchangeable economic laws. The immigrant on the prairie had proven that man could better himself. Misery was not his God-given lot; he was

A Man's Work is Never Done

In the first decade of the twentieth century, men made up almost 90% of the labour force, and in the good years there was no scarcity of jobs. Railways were running spur lines into every town. Gold and silver strikes in Ontario's northland created overnight boomtowns where men who could "tough it" could make a comfortable living. The timber businesses of British Columbia called for loggers from the East. Prairie wheatland needed harvesters and skilled "engineers" to run new equipment. Ontario and Quebec hydro projects lured men by the trainload to work on construction and putting up power lines. Automobile and farm equipment factories advertised for skilled mechanics and craftsmen. The opportunities were limitless. Even if wages were low, a man could feed his family and still have a bit left over for a few luxuries if he kept down a steady job. Here are some of the jobs that grandfather used to do.

Cobourg, Ontario's W.R. Thompson deals in all manner of leather goods, from complete harnesses for horses to boots and gloves for his two-legged customers.

These two foundry workers keep their distance from the heat while tapping this blast furnace at Deloro, Ont. Their clothing alone offers little protection.

Oil can in hand and wearing a brand new pair of coveralls, John Duncan poses "proud as punch" alongside his gleaming steam-powered truck in Victoria, B.C.

Cedars the size of the steam engine are hauled from the B.C. woods. By the end of the decade the province's timber industry was booming and spreading prosperity.

Hats and overalls separate workers from supervisors among this crew bonding a pipeline on a 1904 Ontario power project. The boater and tie seem out of place.

Any street corner will do for St. John, N.B.'s Charlie Brown, the local shoe-shine "boy." A spit and polish cost you 10 cents, and his hat says "no credit."

**Herbert Holt
The Billion-Dollar Recluse**

Money and power were Herbert
Holt's passion, his yardstick of
success, and he succeeded wildly. His
name alone became so powerful that
when rumours of his dealings on the
stock exchange became known, prices
sky-rocketed or plummeted. He came
to Canada from Ireland in 1875, at
19, trained as a civil engineer, and
worked till 1901 supervising railway
construction. Then he moved his home
to Montreal and began making money
in earnest. He headed the Royal Bank
until his death in 1941, built up the
world's largest privately-owned
utility, bought Anticosti Island for
its forests, became a shareholder
in more than 300 companies on four
continents, and headed 27 major corporations. Cold and reclusive, he had
few friends during his lifetime.

free to change his circumstances. The fast-growing
grain growers' co-ops, which in time would lead to
the CCF party, were a protest against the belief that
things had to stay the way they were. The instinc-
tive urge for freedom that had begun the quest for
free land was becoming a force for reform.

Prices were rising and wages were not, adding
fuel to the discontent. In 1910 there were sixty-
seven strikes. And when Grand Trunk president
Charlie Hays forced a railway strike that year,
Laurier wired his new labour minister, thirty-five-
year-old Mackenzie King: "I am deluged with te-
legrams asking me to interfere."

a time for heretics

Interference with business was heresy but it
was a time for heretics. As a young reporter,
Mackenzie King had helped to clean up sweatshops, and under Sir William Mulock, Laurier's
postmaster-general, he had organized a department of labour in 1900. In 1907 he had drawn up
the Industrial Disputes Investigation Act, which
called for the arbitration of strikes in quasi-public
industries – an experiment, noted O.D. Skelton,
that "awakened world-wide interest." In 1910
King introduced the Combines Investigation Act.
From now on, business magnates would be har-
assed by government, public opinion and labour.

The International Workers of the World – "the
Wobblies" – had been formed in the United States
in 1905 and had started to organize in the Canadian West. The IWW constitution stated that "the
working class and the employing class have nothing in common." By 1910, however, the crude
"assembly line" would prove them wrong. The
idea of mass production gave birth to a new
thought: that the more a factory produces the
more it can pay its workers, that the more a
worker earns the more he buys, and the more he
buys the cheaper the goods produced.

At the same time the cost of machine tools was
calling for volume sales and capital, and was thus
pushing firms toward merger and monopoly. Max
Aitken – later Lord Beaverbrook – put together
Canada Cement and the Steel Company of Canada. Herbert Holt merged eighteen firms into
Montreal Light, Heat & Power. Charles Gordon
created Dominion Textile from a group of textile
companies. In 1910, thirty-four factories of Canadian Canners were merged with fourteen independent companies to form Dominion Canners
Limited. The Canadian Bank of Commerce ab-
sorbed the Bank of British Columbia, and the
Royal Bank took over the Union Bank of Halifax.
The twenty-two mergers that took place in 1910
were capitalized at $157 million.

electrical inventions

The machine, harnessed to waterpower, had
begun to emancipate women. By 1910 they could
make a pound of ice in an hour with the one-
horsepower Brunswick refrigerator. They could
cook with thirty switches and plugs on a General
Electric range, although it was still a copy of a
wood stove. And as early as 1907 the Edison Company was advertising the first clumsy prototypes of
an electric vacuum cleaner, frying "kettle," waffle
iron, clothes washer and wringer, sewing machine,
silver buffer and dishwasher.

The new machines were reshaping a way of
life. The electric tram, or trolley, was expanding
the city suburbs, "creating," as one writer put it,
"thousands of healthful homes." The gas engine
was taking fishermen farther afield, and trains
were hauling cod and salmon in the new refriger-
ated cars across the country at almost a mile a
minute. The iron chink, a machine for beheading
and gutting fish, introduced in west coast canneries in 1906, had begun the trend toward automa-
tion in industry. And by 1910 car makers were

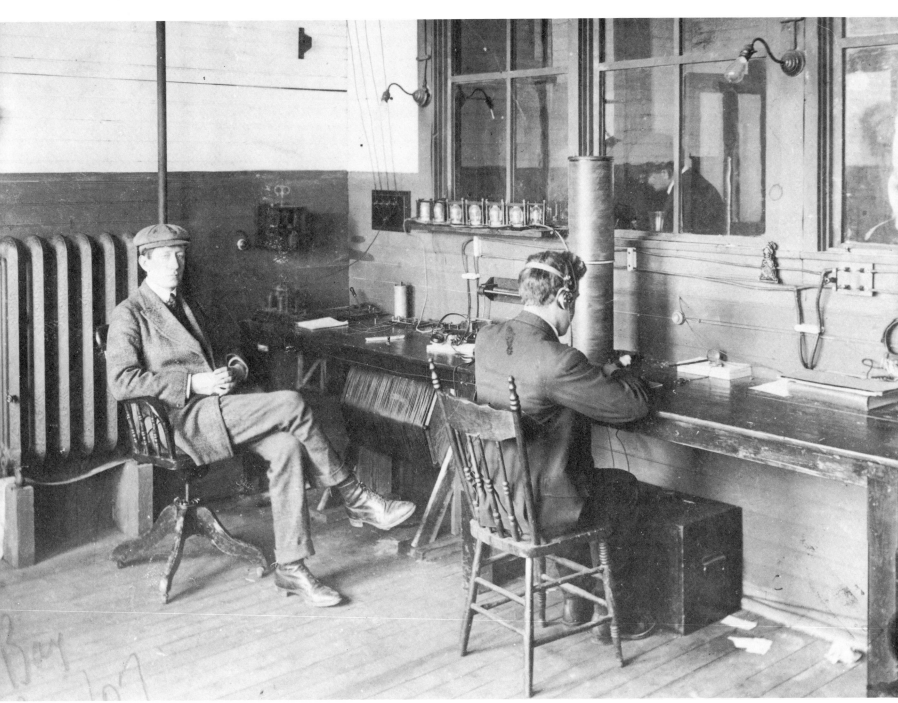

Marconi (left) watches operations in the receiving room of the Marconi Wireless Telegraph Co. in Glace Bay, N.S., as the first commercial press message passes through.

119

A Dazzling Array of Gadgets

Gadgets, gadgets, and more gadgets tumbled from inventors' drawing boards, factories, and store shelves. Electric hearing aids plucked sound fom the air. Vacuum cleaners began sucking dirt from underfoot in 1901, then went portable in 1905. A Norwegian invented the postage meter. Long play records gave drawing room music buffs longer passages from light opera like "Bohemian Girl" and "Poet and Peasant" – 12 minutes' worth. An American invented paper cups. Autos were improved with four-wheel brakes and electric headlights. Electric washing machines took some of the aches out of Mondays, and the new safety razors began stroking stubbled cheeks in the morning. And, from 1906, photocopiers helped out at the office.

The phonograph horn was soon replaced by internal speakers.

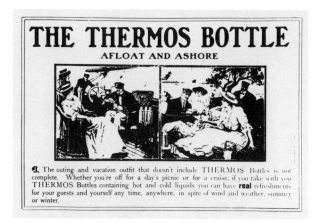

THE THERMOS BOTTLE
AFLOAT AND ASHORE

The outing and vacation outfit that doesn't include THERMOS Bottles is not complete. Whether you're off for a day's picnic or for a cruise, if you take with you THERMOS Bottles containing hot and cold liquids you can have **real** refreshments for your guests and yourself any time, anywhere, in spite of wind and weather, summer or winter.

Hot soup on a picnic? What'll they think of next?

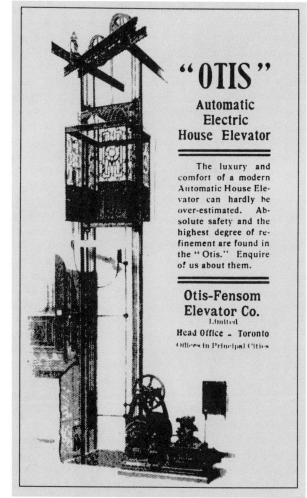

"OTIS"
Automatic Electric House Elevator

The luxury and comfort of a modern Automatic House Elevator can hardly be over-estimated. Absolute safety and the highest degree of refinement are found in the "Otis." Enquire of us about them.

Otis-Fensom Elevator Co.
Limited
Head Office - Toronto
Offices in Principal Cities

The idling rich took their ups and downs in style.

"Hotpoint"

Smooth out wrinkles with electricity.

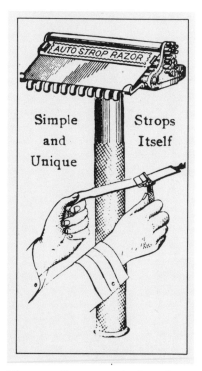

AUTO STROP RAZOR

Simple and Unique

Strops Itself

The new safety razor gained an edge.

This camera used glass plates, rather than rolls of film.

Many early player pianos could also be played by hand.

Early pens were filled with eyedroppers.

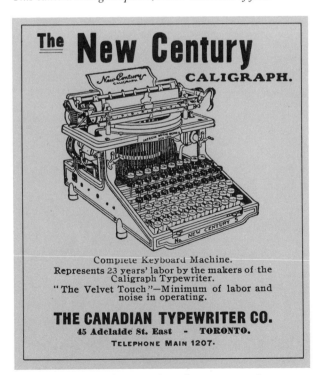
Better look again. This is a caligraph, not a typewriter.

By the end of the decade, these came with motors attached.

These would crowd most bathrooms.

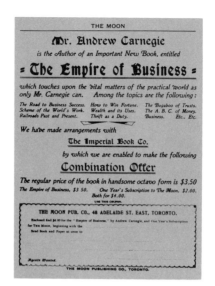

*American success stories, business
methods and financial gospels found
a ready market among Canadians, but
there's probably no mention in* The
Empire of Business *that Mr. Carnegie
was swindled out of $250,000 by the
notorious Cassie Chadwick from
Eastwood, Ontario in 1904.*

changing the concept of machining, shrinking the
margin of tolerance for precision tools.

By now technology had become the handmai-
den of business. In Sault Ste. Marie Ernest Arthur
LeSueur, a chemical engineer who had liquefied
natural gas for storage in 1903, was producing the
first TNT made in Canada; in St. Catharines, Ontario, Gideon Sundback was working on the zip-
per. Near Thetford, Quebec, H.J. Johns was exploring new uses for asbestos.

New products were revamping the economy.
In 1910 the first man-made fibre, rayon or
"artificial silk," came on the North American market, spreading the irreverent idea that man could
better nature. Bakelite, custom-made from chemi-
cals, had appeared in 1909, another "plastic" material like celluloid. Kits for iron and basketwork
had begun the do-it-yourself business. The pay
phone and the paper cup dispenser, grown out of
an Egyptian device for dispensing holy water, had
begun the vending machine business.

New products called for new sales techniques. A
1910 article on advertising spelled out the new creed:
*Modern advertising is not merely a method of divert-
ing trade away from the merchant or manufacturer
who does not advertise . . . it actually creates business
that would not have been. . . . Advertising sold the Ko-
dak and the car, "all-wool" clothing, steam radiators,
safety razors, brand-name flour . . . it multiplies human wants and intensifies desires [and] impels a man
to greater buying. To buy more he must earn more. It
therefore inevitably increases his productivity . . .*

The individualistic society now had a new
common denominator, a goal for both sexes, for
the rich and the poor, for nation and individual:
the gospel of productivity. It would do more to
lower class barriers than two thousand years of
Christian preaching.

The nation – all nations – had been groping toward a new faith and they found it in the mechanics of mass production. The assembly line was the
womb of modern society. It prescribed ever-larger
units for efficiency. It implied a total community
as compared to a community where each family
produced its own food and clothing.

The idea of man's perfectibility was becoming
the perfectibility of society. Canada, along with
the rest of the western world, was committed for
good or ill to the concept of progress, to continuous and inevitable growth. It was the logical out-
come of Edwardian optimism, that irrational faith
in man's rationality.

*Are these the faces of bank robbers or
cautious depositers? Judging by the
smiles on the tellers' faces, they're
likely solid citizens of Cobourg, Ont.*

No, this is not a chorus line but the fabulous Renfrew Millionaires hockey team of 1909. It's hard to believe that these were the toughest bruisers in the early days of the game; (left to right) Bobby Rowe, Herb Jordan, Fred Whitcroft, Newsy Lalonde, Cyclone Taylor, Frank Patrick, Larry Filmor and Lester Patrick.

Acknowledgements

This book took shape in the Toronto Central Reference Library, in my browsing among the papers and periodicals of the period: the Toronto *Globe, Mail and Empire, Saturday Night, The Canadian Magazine, Canadian Home Journal, Canadian Courier,* and above all, *Maclean's,* which evolved in 1907 from *Busy Man's Magazine.* It wasn't a national magazine yet, but it was the closest thing to it, and for me, the most rewarding source of material.

The journalists gave me the feel of the decade and what they considered the main events; the historians gave me perspective and detail. I wish I had space to acknowledge my debt to the authors of all the books I consulted but the list runs long: counting biographers and autobiographers, more than sixty.

Lastly, I owe thanks to my elders who relived the decade for me, in particular my father, Fred Phillips, whose railway survey team put some towns on the map of the prairies in the manner described in the chapter on western settlement.

Alan Phillips

The Author

Alan Phillips was raised in Southampton Ontario, studied commercial art and business, then began a varied career in the working world: he was a lifeguard in Florida, a ranchhand in Texas, an insurance investigator, and a boatman on Ontario's Avon River. He served in the Royal Canadian Navy during World War II, then joined the National Film Board as producer and writer, and has been free-lancing since 1951. He broadcast a CBC radio program on business for five years; wrote film and TV scripts, government pamphlets, radio documentaries and articles for *Maclean's, National Geographic, Weekend, Argosy,* and other magazines. *The Living Legend,* his book on the RCMP, was widely acclaimed.

124

Index

The page numbers in italics refer to illustrations and captions

Picture Credits

In 1972.

Visitor from the Province
of Pennsylvania:
"Who are these curiously dressed
old men I see in your streets?"

Fair Ontario Girl:
"Oh, they are some of the Canadian
Mounted Rifles who returned from
South Africa in 1902."

We would like to acknowledge the help and cooperation of the directors and staff of the various public institutions and the private firms and individuals who made available paintings, posters, mementoes, collections and albums as well as photographs and gave us permission to reproduce them. Every effort has been made to identify and credit appropriately the sources of all illustrations used in this book. Any further information will be appreciated and acknowledged in subsequent editions.

The illustrations are listed in the order of their appearance on the page, left to right, top to bottom. Principal sources are credited under these abbreviations:

PAC   Public Archives of Canada
MTCL   Metropolitan Toronto Central Library
PABC   Provincial Archives, Victoria, B.C.
GA   Glenbow-Alberta Institute
KML   Killam Memorial Library, Dalhousie University Archives

UCA   The Archives of the United Church of Canada /1 MTCL /2 Massey Ferguson Ltd; The Globe /4 private collection /6 Wilson Studio, St. John, N.B. /7 Alan Suddon /8 Hastings County Historical Society /9 PABC S3243 /10 Provincial Archives of Alberta /11 private collection /12 Fenelon Falls County Museum; Wilson Studio, St. John, N.B. /13 Wilson Studio, St. John N.B.; Public Archives of Nova Scotia /14 Provincial Archives of Alberta, E. Brown Collection /15 Vancouver Public Library; James Collection – City of Toronto Archives; Archives, Eaton's of Canada; Archives, Eaton's of Canada /16 Vancouver Public Library /17 Culver Pictures /18 PAC C14090; Sports Hall of Fame /19 PAC C22771; City of Victoria Archives /20 The Habitant, W. H. Drummond; The Biography of a Grizzly /21 MTCL;MTCL;MTCL; Yukon Archives Library Services Branch YTG #4534 /22 private collection; Nova Scotia Museum, Halifax, N.S.; Nova Scotia Museum, Halifax, N.S. /23 Nova Scotia Museum, Halifax, N.S.; private collection /24 private collection /25 Public Archives of Ontario /26 PAC C932 /27 Who's Who, Canadian Publications /28 Public Archives of Ontario /29 Fenelon Falls Museum /30 Saskatchewan Archives Photograph /31 MTCL /32 Saturday Night 1903; MTCL; Saturday Night 1903 /33 PAC /34 KML; KML /35 KML; private collection /36 Provincial Archives of Manitoba /37 PAC C52819 /38 Wilson Studio, St. John, N.B. /39 PAC C22944 /40 PAC C5130; PAC PA11514; GA /41 Saskat-

chewan Archives Photograph; PAC C5611 /42 PAC C5093; Saskatchewan Archives Photograph /43 Saskatchewan Archives; Koozma Tarasoff Collection – PABC /44 and 45 Manitoba Archives /46 and 47 W.O. Buchanan, MTCL /48 PABC /49 MTCL /50 MTCL; CN Archives; The Moon /51 Notman Photographic Archives /52 Maclean's /53 Quebec Literary and Historical Society /54 PAC C 17582 /55 GA; The Railway and Marine World /56 Kings College /57 McGill Yearbook /58 and 59 private collection /60 PABC /61 University of Alberta Archives 60-12-224 /62 University of Alberta Archives; PAC PA 13012 /63 University of Alberta; Ontario Ladies College /64 Old McGill; private collection /65 private collection /66 Eaton's Archives; private collection /67 Nova Scotia Museum /68 Canadian Automotive Museum /69 Motoring /70 MTCL; PAC C3002 /71 James Collection – City of Toronto Archives; Ontario Motor League /72 W.H. McCurdy, Petheric Press; Vancouver Public Archives /73 GA /74 J.V. Salmon /75 Ontario Motor League; Ontario Motor League /76 Saturday Night Scrapbook /77 S.J. Hayward Photography /78 private collection; PABC; GA /79 Foote Collection, Manitoba Archives; Archives Nationales du Quebec; Peterborough County Museum /80 The Cobalt Mining Museum Collection, Archives of Ontario /81 MTCL /82 H. Peters Collection, Public Archives of Ontario /83 Ontario Archives /84 Hollinger Mines; Ontario Archives /85 PAC C22982; The Cobalt Mining Museum Collection, Archives of Ontario /86 Ontario Archives /87 The Cobalt Mining Museum Collection, Archives of Ontario /88 Maclean Hunter /89 private collection /90 PAC C5640; MTCL Fine Art Dept, Pat Rogal /91 MTCL Fine Art Dept, Pat Rogal /92 Library of Congress /93 Allan Suddon /94 Frank Ellis /95 Bettman Archives, Inc. /96 Canada's Flying Heritage /97 Library of Congress; National Geographic Society, Washington, D.C. /98 MTCL /99 Saskatchewan Archives /100 Public Archives of Ontario /101 UCA /102 PAC C858880 /103 UCA; UCA /104 UCA; Foote Collection, Manitoba Archives /105 Manitoba Archives; UCA /106 James Collection – City of Toronto Archives /107 UCA; Geological Survey of Canada, Ottawa /108 Ontario Hydro /109 I.O.F. /110 and 111 Eaton's Archives /112 MTCL Fine Art Dept. Pat Rogal /113 private collection /114 GA; GA /115 Archives Nationales du Quebec; The Queen's Own Rifles of Canada, Regimental Museum, Calgary, Alberta /116 Public Archives of Ontario; Deloro Stellite, Division of Canadian Oxygen Limited /117 PABC; Ontario Hydro; Canadian Pacific; Wilson Collection (Erb Negatives) /118 The Royal Bank Archives /119 Nova Scotia Museum, Halifax, N.S. /120 MTCL; MTCL; MTCL; PABC; MTCL /121 MTCL; MTCL; Canada Monthly; The National Monthly Advertiser; MTCL; MTCL /122 The Moon /123 British Columbia Sports Hall of Fame.